MUSIC MANIA!

Trivia lovers, it's time to face the music! So tune up your musical expertise and get into the trivia rhythm with this prelude:

1. Who sang the sound track for the film *The Graduate*?
2. What great musical producer and songwriter was crippled in a riding accident?
3. What was the Beatles' biggest hit single?
4. What is Satchmo's real name?
5. What male vocalist sang the theme for the movie *Ghostbusters*?
6. Who wrote the Peter, Paul and Mary hit "Leaving on a Jet Plane"?
7. What was the name of the small town where *The Music Man* took place?
8. Who was the first star to have six singles from the same album reach the top ten?
9. Name the famous songwriter who wrote "White Christmas."
10. What genuine sister group recorded "Yes We Can Can" and "He's So Shy"?

For the answers to these and 990 others, keep on reading. Surrender yourself to a symphony of tuneful teasers and become the #1 hit of TRIVIA MANIA!

TRIVIA MANIA
by Xavier Einstein

TRIVIA MANIA has arrived! With enough questions to answer every trivia buff's dreams, TRIVIA MANIA covers it all—from the delightfully obscure to the seemingly obvious. Tickle your fancy, and test your memory!

MUSIC

TRIVIA Mania

BY XAVIER EINSTEIN

ZEBRA BOOKS
KENSINGTON PUBLISHING CORP.

The author wishes to thank Linda and Barry Stuart and Bette and Dale Rupert for their work on this book.

ZEBRA BOOKS

are published by

Kensington Publishing Corp.
475 Park Avenue South
New York, N.Y. 10016

First printing: August, 1984

Printed in the United States of America

TRIVIA MANIA:
Music

1) In 1968 what group recorded *Safe as Milk*?

2) What band was one of the first to do outrageous acts on stage and had a hit with "School's Out"?

3) What middle-aged lady became famous in 1966 for not being able to sing?

4) Named after either Dorothy's dog or lead vocalist Bobby Kimball's surname (Toteaux), which group had the hit "Rosanna" and won seven 1983 Grammys?

5) Who played George Cohan in the 1968 musical *George M*?

6) True or false: *Rolling Stone* magazine was originated by the group of the same name.

. . . Answers

1. Captain Beefheart and His Magic Band

2. Alice Cooper

3. Mrs. (Elva) Miller

4. Toto

5. Joel Grey

6. False

7) What Broadway musical was Rodgers & Hammerstein's final collaboration?

8) Fritz Reiner conducted which major orchestra?

9) Her recording of "I'm Sorry" was #1 on the charts for three weeks in 1960. Name her.

10) Brothers Johnny and Edgar have nearly twenty R & B albums between them, but only one, *Together Live*, was recorded together. What's their last name?

11) Who was the original Maria on Broadway in 1957's *West Side Story*?

12) What female rock 'n' roll singer had a filigree-style bracelet tattooed on her wrist and a tattoo over her heart?

13) What English group recorded *Days of Future Passed* and *In Search of the Lost Chord*?

14) "I'm Not in Love" and "The Things We Do for Love" were top ten hits for which British group whose tenth album was *Ten Out of Ten*?

15) Who is the woman who recorded "I Am Woman"?

16) What group touring with the Cars in 1984 remembers "Those Dance Hall Days" in song and video?

. . . Answers

7. *The Sound of Music*

8. Chicago Symphony Orchestra

9. Brenda Lee

10. Winter

11. Carol Lawrence

12. Janis Joplin

13. The Moody Blues

14. 10cc

15. Helen Reddy

16. Wang Chung

QUESTIONS

17) Which musical play starred Richard Burton as Arthur in 1960?

18) What entertainer is allowing one of his songs to be used in a government campaign to beat drunk driving?

19) He was known as "Daddy Bluegrass." Bluegrass music got its name from his band. Who is he?

20) Who were Bill Medley and Bobby Hatfield better known as?

21) What was Ishkabibble's real name?
   a. George Dexter
   b. D.S. (Pops) Stuart
   c. Merwyn Bogue
   d. Bill Pulin

22) What Canadian soul singer did the vocals for Blood, Sweat and Tears starting with their second album in 1978?

23) Who sang "Moon River" and earned a gold record for it in 1961?

24) Who wrote the Ricky Nelson hit "I'm Walkin' ":
   a. Shakin' Stevens
   b. Cat Stevens
   c. Fats Domino
   d. Brian Hyland

. . . *Answers*

17. *Camelot*

18. Michael Jackson

19. Bill Monroe

20. The Righteous Brothers

21. c

22. David Clayton-Thomas

23. Andy Williams

24. c

QUESTIONS

25) What do the following musicians have in common: Zal Yanovsky (Lovin' Spoonful), Denny Doherty (Mamas and the Papas) and Gordon Lightfoot?

26) What band recorded the 1978 hit album *Briefcase Full of Blues*?

27) True or false: The song "Over the Rainbow" was almost cut from *The Wizard of Oz*.

28) True or false: Two of the Bee Gees are twins.

29) What instruments make up a classical bluegrass band?

30) What female trio sang "Robert De Niro's Waiting"?

31) Who sang such protest songs as "Universal Soldier" and "My Country 'Tis of Thy People You're Dying"?

32) What Canadian band projects images of the sci-fi future and recorded the albums *2112* and *Rush Through Time*?

33) What was the name of the white gang in the musical *West Side Story*?

34) What's the name of Burt Bacharach's most celebrated lyric writer?

. . . Answers

25. All are from Canada

26. The Blues Brothers

27. True

28. True

29. Guitar, fiddle, mandolin, bass and banjo

30. Bananarama

31. Buffy Sainte-Marie

32. Rush

33. Jets

34. Hal David

35) What group created the rock opera *Tommy* about a deaf, dumb and blind boy?

36) First name is Grover. Instruments include jazz flute and piano as well as soprano, tenor and baritone saxes. Who is he?

37) According to *Cashbox* what was the #1 single of 1963?
    a. "Fingertips (Part 2)"
    b. "Telstar"
    c. "Limbo Rock"

38) What hippie comic team recorded the Motown cut "Does Your Mama Know About Me"?

39) "Shop Around" by the Miracles was the first million-seller of what famous record label?

40) Who played harmonica on Harry Belafonte's song "Midnight Special"?

41) Which of the following plays was not a biography?
    a. *Gypsy*
    b. *Cindy*
    c. *Funny Girl*

42) One of the Monkees wrote Linda Ronstadt's first hit, "Different Drum". True or false?

43) Who sang "A Boy Named Sue"?

... Answers

35. The Who

36. Grover Washington, Jr.

37. c

38. Cheech and Chong

39. Motown

40. Bob Dylan

41. b

42. True. It was written by Mike Nesmith.

43. Johnny Cash

44) Who is the acclaimed jazz-rock fusion guitarist who did the album *Standing Ovation*?
    a. Larry Coryell
    b. Al DiMeola
    c. Paul Skalicky
    d. John McLaughlin

45) What pair announced the upcoming birth of their first child to a full house at Madison Square Garden in 1968? (Sadly, they lost the child.)

46) What group in 1972 was aboard the *Hellbound Train*?

47) True or false: The British male singer who sang under the name Cliff Richard was really named Hardy Webb.

48) Under what name did Donald Fagen and Walter Becker have the top twenty hits "Reelin' in the Years" and "Rikki Don't Lose That Number"?

49) This Broadway star, movie star, scholar and country music star was born in 1907 in Panola County, east Texas. Who is he?

50) Ritchie Blackmore was the guitarist for what British rock band that did "Hush" and "Smoke on the Water"?

. . . Answers

44. a

45. Sonny and Cher

46. Savoy Brown

47. True

48. Steely Dan

49. Tex Ritter

50. Deep Purple

QUESTIONS

Match the play with the year

51)	*Funny Girl*	a.	1968
52)	*Cabaret*	b.	1964
53)	*Zorba*	c.	1966
54)	*Hair*	d.	1965
55)	*Do I Hear a Waltz?*	e.	1967

56) Who recorded the official song of the Middle Tennessee Teamsters Union, "Take This Job and Shove It"?

57) Which of the following is an English group named after a Robert Benton western?
    a. Bad Company
    b. Bad Manners
    c. Badfinger
    d. Cactus

58) True or false: Buffy Sainte-Marie is a Cree Indian.

59) Who had the 1957 smash "Honeycomb"?

60) Who is known as the "Tennessee Plowboy"?

61) Debbie Harry was part of the New York music and art scene and had a hit single called "Rapture." What was the name of her group?

. . . *Answers*

51. b

52. c

53. a

54. e

55. d

56. Johnny Paycheck

57. a

58. True

59. Jimmie Rodgers

60. Eddy Arnold

61. Blondie

62) She was born Wynette Pugh in 1942. Her first #1 single was "I Don't Wanna Play House." Who is she?

63) Poetry books *The Lords* and *The New Creatures* were written by what rock star?
   a. Jim Morrison
   b. George Harrison
   c. Bob Dylan

64) In 1966 what group introduced a dance named after their leader?

65) On the piano, the left hand typically plays the bass clef. What does the right hand play?

66) What distinctively named trumpet player was a member of Kay Kyser's band?

67) "He's So Fine," "One Fine Day" and "A Love So Fine" were hits for what fine-fabric group?

68) Through 1963 this duo's total record sales exceeded eighteen million with successes including "Cathy's Clown" and "Wake Up, Little Susie." Who are they?

69) What band recorded "Give Peace a Chance"?

70) The songs "One" and "What I Did For Love" came from what Broadway musical?

. . . *Answers*

62. Tammy Wynette

63. a

64. Freddie and the Dreamers

65. Treble clef

66. Ishkabibble

67. The Chiffons

68. The Everly Brothers

69. The Plastic Ono Band

70. *A Chorus Line*

71) True or false: Gladys Knight won the Ted Mack Original Amateur Hour at age eight.

72) What sixties group recorded "On the Road Again"?

73) Who recorded the 1978 hit "Three Times a Lady"?

74) What country musician recorded "Before the Next Teardrop Falls"?

75) True or false: Gary, of Gary Lewis and the Playboys, is the son of comedian Jerry Lewis.

76) True or false: Paul McCartney wrote "World Without Love," which was later recorded by Peter and Gordon.

77) Ian Anderson is the lead singer for what English group? They produced the successful *Aqualung* album.

78) True or false: Superman was at one time a Broadway play.

79) How many gold records have been awarded to the Beatles?
   a. twelve
   b. twenty-one
   c. thirty-three
   d. forty-three

. . . Answers

71. True

72. Canned Heat

73. The Commodores

74. Freddy Fender

75. True

76. True

77. Jethro Tull

78. True

79. d

80) From what play did the song "Climb Every Mountain" come?

81) What Motown group recorded "Baby I Need Your Loving" in 1964 and "Reach Out and I'll Be There" in 1966?

82) Who sang the soundtrack for the film *The Graduate*?

83) Wilton Felder on reeds and Joe Sample on keyboards make up the Crusaders. What was the group's original name?

84) Dean Torrence and Jan Berry's recordings embraced the sixties California trilogy of beach, sea and freeways. What name did they record under?

85) "Cry Like a Baby" was a 1968 hit for what Memphis soul band?

86) He was known for his Latin music and his wives: Carmen, Lorain, Abbe Lane, and Charo. Who is he?

87) "Joy to the World" was a hit in 1971 for what band with three lead vocalists?

88) Which of these albums was ranked #1 in 1965?
   a. *Beach Boys Today*
   b. *Mary Poppins*
   c. *People*

. . . Answers

80. *The Sound of Music*

81. The Four Tops

82. Simon and Garfunkel

83. The Jazz Crusaders

84. Jan and Dean

85. The Box Tops

86. Xavier Cugat

87. Three Dog Night

88. b

89) Her 1983 album *What's New* is actually a collection of early twentieth century standards backed up by the Nelson Riddle orchestra. Who is she?

90) Neil Simon adapted *Sweet Charity* from what motion picture?

91) Who was the renowned conductor of the New York Philharmonic Orchestra?

92) Which play ran the longest on Broadway?
   a. *Hello Dolly*
   b. *Fiddler on the Roof*
   c. *Funny Girl*

93) Fifties rock 'n' roll was revived in the seventies by what greased hair, T-shirted, TV-frequenting group?

94) What was the name of the album the Rolling Stones recorded in answer to the Beatles' *Sergeant Pepper*?

95) Who led Mad Dogs and Englishmen, Joe Cocker's former touring band, and wrote "Delta Lady"?

96) Which country performer was given a one-to-fifteen year sentence for burglary?

. . . Answers

89. Linda Ronstadt

90. *The Nights of Cabiria*

91. Arturo Toscanini

92. b

93. Sha-Na-Na

94. *Their Satanic Majesties Request*

95. Leon Russell

96. Merle Haggard

97) Which of the following was Patti Page's hit single in 1951?

    a. "Fever"
    b. "Over the Rainbow"
    c. "Summertime"
    d. "Tennessee Waltz"

98) Who starred with Barbra Streisand in the 1976 movie *A Star Is Born*?

99) Who worked as Carole King's babysitter and also had the hit song "The Loco-Motion"?

100) What famous classical composer continued to compose great music after becoming deaf?

Match the song with the musical

101) "Marion the Librarian"	a. *Camelot*
102) "Lusty Day of May"	b. *Annie Get Your Gun*
103) "Anything You Can Do"	c. *Hello Dolly*
104) "Before the Parade Passes By"	d. *The Music Man*
105) "Brush Up Your Shakespeare"	e. *Kiss Me Kate*

. . . Answers

97. d

98. Kris Kristofferson

99. Little Eva

100. Ludwig Von Beethoven

101. d

102. a

103. b

104. c

105. e

QUESTIONS

106) In the US, a platinum album is one that has sold at least what?
    a. two million dollars worth of records
    b. one million dollars worth of records
    c. one million copies
    d. two million copies

107) In what year did Deep Purple release their first album, *Shades of Deep Purple*?

108) The top and bottom strings on a standard guitar are two octaves apart and tuned to what note?

109) One or another of this recording artist's records was number one on the top ten for twenty-five of the fifty-two weeks of 1956. Who is he?

110) What is unusual about the rock group Spinal Tap?

111) In the late fifties who sang such tunes as "Teenage Crush" and "Cutie Wootie"? He was also married to Nancy Sinatra for a short time.

112) The single cutaway Les Paul guitar is a well-known model from what company?
    a. Fender
    b. Gibson
    c. Gretsch
    d. Epiphone

. . . *Answers*

106. c

107. 1968

108. E

109. Elvis Presley

110. It is a fictitious movie-created group

111. Tommy Sands

112. b

113) He is a former Rhodes Scholar, a writer, singer and actor. Who is he?

114) What male singer wrote the McDonald's advertising song "You Deserve a Break Today"?

115) Mary Martin's most famous TV role was done in 1954. What was it?

116) What American songwriter and producer wrote "To Know Him Is to Love Him"?
    a. Neil Sedaka
    b. Phil Spector
    c. Jackie DeShannon
    d. Rita Coolidge

117) Who was lead singer of the Jeff Beck Group that recorded the albums *Truth* and *Beck-Ola*?

118) The gold record "Baby, I'm-A Want You" was recorded by what group?

119) The Weavers' hit "Goodnight Irene" was written by whom?

120) This group is successful even though two of its original members have died. They had the 1980 hit "Talk of the Town." Who are they?

121) True or false: McCartney and Lennon produced a stage musical.

. . . *Answers*

113. Kris Kristofferson

114. Barry Manilow

115. Peter Pan

116. b

117. Rod Stewart

118. Bread

119. Leadbelly (Huddie Ledbetter)

120. The Pretenders

121. False

QUESTIONS

122) What female vocalist and songwriter followed the "White Rabbit" to success?

123) She starred in *West Side Story* as Anita and in *Bye Bye Birdie* as Rose. What is her name?

124) What English-born conductor starred in the musical films *One Hundred Men and a Girl* and *Fantasia*?

125) This female artist enjoyed success on both popular and country & western stations with such tunes as "Let Me Be There" and "Have You Never Been Mellow."

126) Whose father sits at night with no lights on?

127) What is the relationship between the singing team of Royce and Jeannie Kendall?

128) Who wrote the Byrds' hits "Turn Turn Turn" and "The Bells of Rhymney"?

129) Who is known as "The Pride of Country Music"?

130) What was the Beatles' biggest hit single?

131) Who was the founder of the Lovin' Spoonful and also wrote several songs for *Jimmy Shine*, a Broadway musical starring Dustin Hoffman?

. . . *Answers*

122. Grace Slick

123. Chita Rivera

124. Leopold Stokowski

125. Olivia Newton-John

126. Carly Simon

127. Father and daughter

128. Pete Seeger

129. Charley Pride

130. "Hey Jude"

131. John Sebastian

132) How many sharps are there in the key of D?
    a. none
    b. one
    c. two
    d. three

133) What country recording star was married to George Jones?

134) The book *In His Own Write* was written by what rock star?
    a. John Lennon
    b. George Harrison
    c. Bob Dylan

135) Name the clean-cut, wholesome, very happily married singer who is known for his white shoes.

136) What Boston rock band recorded "Shake It Up" in 1982?

137) Who became the third British group to have a #1 record in the U.S. when they released "Do Wah Diddy Diddy" in 1964?

138) How many copies of a 45 rpm single must be sold for it to earn a gold record in the U.S.?

139) Who referred to his group as "The Malted Milk Band"?

. . . Answers

132. c

133. Tammy Wynette

134. a

135. Pat Boone

136. The Cars

137. Manfred Mann

138. One million

139. Les Brown

140) What group had to change their name from the comic-strip character Pogo and had the 1979 hit "Heat of the Night"?

141) Who was named Best New Artist by the National Academy of Recording Arts and Science in 1962?

142) In 1966 who recorded "Don't Be a Drop-Out" for the Office of Economic Opportunity?

143) Blind boy Grunt was a fictional singer created by what songwriter/singer?

144) What is Satchmo's real name?

145) What singer-songwriter had one of his songs, "Distant Drums," reach #1 on the English charts three years after his death?

146) What sweet-voiced singer recorded the hit song "Angel of the Morning"?

147) True or false: Mitch Ryder and the Detroit Wheels used to be called Billy Lee and the Rivieras.

148) What group, one of the world's biggest, had the hits "Every Breath You Take" and "Wrapped Around Your Finger"?

149) True or false: The Gentrys, of "Keep On Dancing" fame, included Bobbie Gentry on guitar.

. . . Answers

140. Poco

141. Robert Goulet

142. James Brown

143. Bob Dylan

144. Louis Armstrong

145. Jim Reeves

146. Merrilee Rush

147. True

148. The Police

149. False

QUESTIONS

150) What male vocalist sang the theme for the movie *Ghostbusters*?

Match the play with the year

151) *Hello Dolly*	a.	1966
152) *Guys and Dolls*	b.	1964
153) *Gentlemen Prefer Blondes*	c.	1953
154) *Sweet Charity*	d.	1956
155) *Li'l Abner*	e.	1950

156) Who was the star of the all-black version of *Hello Dolly*?

157) True or false: The Isley Brothers, Ronald, Rudolph and O'Kelly, are not really brothers.

158) What label was Loretta Lynn's "I'm a Honky Tonk Girl" recorded on?

159) What male vocalist sang "Venus"?
   a. Bobby Darin
   b. Frank Sinatra
   c. Howlin' Wolf
   d. Frankie Avalon

160) Who was the singer in the Hare Trigger Band?

. . . *Answers*

150. Ray Parker, Jr.

151. b

152. e

153. c

154. a

155. d

156. Pearl Bailey

157. False

158. Zero (her own label)

159. d

160. Eddie Rabbitt

161) What disc jockey is credited with coining the phrase "rock 'n' roll"?
    a. Doug Hamilton
    b. Alan Freed
    c. K J Grunstra
    d. Willy the "K"

162) In 1968 what singer released her biggest hit, "Both Sides Now"?

163) Who sang "Georgia on My Mind" and "One Mint Julep"?

164) Mr. Leitch recorded "Sunshine Superman" and "Mellow Yellow" under what name?

165) Which is not part of a violin bow?
    a. nut
    b. frog
    c. goat

166) Who recorded "Only the Lonely," "Crying" and "Oh Pretty Woman"?

167) What Scottish vocalist was Britain's "answer" to Bob Dylan?

168) True or false: Rodgers and Hammerstein are step-brothers.

. . . Answers

161. b

162. Judy Collins

163. Ray Charles

164. Donovan

165. c

166. Roy Orbison

167. Donovan

168. False

169) How many gold record awards have Elvis Presley's works received?
- a. five
- b. thirteen
- c. twenty-five
- d. forty
- e. sixty-two

170) According to *Cashbox*, what was the #1 single of 1968?
- a. "Mony Mony"
- b. "Hey Jude"
- c. "Tighten Up"

171) What British group formed in 1970 had the hit "The Boys Are Back in Town" from their 1976 *Jailbreak* album?

172) True or false: The song "The Way We Were" came from the film of the same name.

173) What group uses Roman numerals for its album names?

174) Who sang "Ode to Billie Joe"?

175) Who sang the soundtrack and starred in the movie *To Sir With Love*?
- a. Lulu
- b. Melanie
- c. Budgie

. . . Answers

169. d

170. b

171. Thin Lizzy

172. True

173. Chicago

174. Bobbie Gentry

175. a

176) What was the theme song of the Dorsey Brothers Band?

177) Name the band with the 1982 album *A Flock of Seagulls* and the hit single "I Ran (So Far Away)."

178) Who starred in the film version of Rodgers and Hammerstein's *The King and I*?

179) What album cover featured, along with a photo-montage of a curious crowd, wax models of the singing group?

180) What family group recorded "The Rain, the Park, and Other Things" in 1967?

181) True or false: Johnny Mathis was an outstanding high-jumper at college.

182) The song "Matchmaker, Matchmaker" came from what musical play?

183) What group had the hits "There Is" and "Stay in My Corner"?

184) Who wrote the musical score for the musical play *A Chorus Line*?

185) What rock group's video "Legs" features their noted silver key chain and red roadster?

. . . Answers

176. "Sandman"

177. A Flock of Seagulls

178. Yul Brynner and Deborah Kerr

179. *Sgt. Pepper's Lonely Hearts Club Band*

180. The Cowsills

181. True

182. *Fiddler on the Roof*

183. The Dells

184. Marvin Hamlisch

185. ZZ Top

186) "Hey Paula" was whose first (and almost last) hit?

187) Which of these performers is not blind?
  a. Stevie Wonder
  b. Roy Orbison
  c. Ray Charles
  d. Jose Feliciano

188) Name the singer/songwriter who released "Alice's Restaurant" in the spring of 1967.

189) True or false: The Jingling Johnny or crescent is a Turkish percussion instrument.

190) What Hollywood producer, born in 1894, died in 1973, produced the films *The Wizard of Oz*, *Gigi* and "*Singin' in the Rain*"?

191) Name the keyboard instrument consisting of steam-blown whistles that can be heard over ten miles away.

192) What great composer *Kiss Me Kate* and many others) was crippled in a riding accident which crushed his legs? After many painful operations, he finally had them amputated. He died in 1964 at the age of seventy-three.

. . . *Answers*

186. Paul and Paula

187. b

188. Arlo Guthrie

189. True

190. Arthur Freed

191. Calliope

192. Cole Porter

193) What black rhythm group in 1978 has "Got to Get You Into My Life"?

194) What play was adapted from Thornton Wilder's *The Matchmaker* and featured Carol Channing in the leading role?

195) What guitarist/vocalist recorded "This Masquerade"?

196) Since 1959, "Night Life" has been recorded by more than seventy artists and has sold in excess of thirty million copies. Who wrote it?

197) Neil Sedaka's song "Oh Carole" was written about whom?

198) Peter Townshend, John Entwistle, Keith Moon and Roger Daltrey were better known under what name?

199) Lead by Wayne Shorter on sax and Josef Zawinul on keyboards, the group created the successful album *Mysterious Traveler* in 1974. Name the group.

200) What country star died of a heart attack in 1974 in a Nashville police station while bailing out a friend?

. . . *Answers*

193. Earth, Wind and Fire

194. *Hello Dolly*

195. George Benson

196. Willie Nelson

197. Carole King

198. The Who

199. Weather Report

200. Tex Ritter

Match the singer with the hit

201) "Nine to Five"   a. Olivia Newton-John

202) "Piece of the Sky"   b. Barbra Streisand

203) "Magic"   c. Dolly Parton

204) "The Way We Were" d. Emmylou Harris

205) "Please Mr. Please" e. Crystal Gale

206) Who wrote Peter, Paul and Mary's hit "Leaving on a Jet Plane"?
    a. Neil Diamond
    b. Bo Diddley
    c. Jim Croce
    d. John Denver

207) What is Fabian's last name?

208) *Diamond Dogs* was the 1974 work of whom?

209) Peggy Lee sang for what big band?

210) What was the name of Peter, Paul and Mary's magic dragon?

211) Who was the "Dean of The College of Musical Knowledge"?

. . . Answers

201. c

202. d

203. e

204. b

205. a

206. d

207. Forte

208. David Bowie

209. Benny Goodman's

210. Puff

211. Kay Kyser

212) What was Mungo Jerry's smash hit of the seventies?

    a. "In the Summertime"
    b. "Boys in Love"
    c. "Dancin' Romancin' "
    d. "Outer Reaches"

213) A group calling themselves the Shadows stepped in for Buddy Holly after he was killed in a plane crash in 1959. Who was the lead vocalist of the group?

214) Who was the lead singer of The Union Gap?

215) What albino from Texas went on to greatness with his album *The Progressive Blues Experiment*?

216) "A lady who's sure all that glitters is gold and who is buying a stairway to heaven" is the creation of what early heavy metal group?

217) This singer recorded "Shake," "You Send Me" and "Another Saturday Night." In December of 1964 he was shot and killed by a hotel operator. Name him.

218) What band, after being sued by Mayor Daley, had to change its name?

219) Who was the first artist to successfully audition for the Grand Ole Opry without a major label behind him? His best-known songs are "Waterloo" and "I Washed My Hands in Muddy Water."

. . . Answers

212. a

213. Bobby Vee

214. Gary Puckett

215. Johnny Winter

216. Led Zeppelin

217. Sam Cooke

218. Chicago Transit Authority (shortened to Chicago)

219. Stonewall Jackson

220) What is the name of Marvin Gaye's superlative 1971 album, which he wrote and produced?

221) What famous country star is the cousin of Jerry Lee Lewis?

222) What was Elvis Presley's wife's name?

223) What composer and conductor was assistant conductor of the New York Philharmonic, which later became "his" orchestra?

224) How many Beethoven symphonies are there?

225) Who recorded "Big Bad John" and "P.T. 109"? He also sponsored pork sausage.

226) Who had a 1964 smash hit with their version of "Louie Louie"?

227) What country star was playing electric bass with Buddy Holly in 1959 and was asked to give up his seat on the chartered plane that later crashed, killing everyone on board?

228) What female folksinger made her musical debut at thirteen by playing a Mozart piano concerto with the Denver Symphony Orchestra?

229) What was the name of the play that *My Fair Lady* was adapted from?

. . . *Answers*

230) Name the leader of Earth, Wind and Fire. He also played with Booker T. and the MGs and Ramsey Lewis.

231) What's Fats Domino's real first name?

232) During what decade was the electric bass guitar introduced?
    a. 1930s
    b. 1940s
    c. 1950s
    d. 1960s

233) Name the Oscar-winning composer who wrote the score for *Gone With the Wind*.

234) What rock 'n' roller was born October 8, 1935 in Mississippi, a surviving member of twins?

235) Jay Black led this group when they recorded the #1 song of 1963, "She Cried."

236) What British group is the "Owner of a Lonely Heart"?

237) What country group originally called themselves the Country Cut-Ups?

238) The Mamas and the Papas' hit "Dedicated to the One I Love" was first done by what group?

239) Who is Brenda Gayle Webb?

. . . Answers

230. Maurice White

231. Antoine

232. c

233. Max Steiner

234. Elvis Presley

235. Jay and the Americans

236. Yes

237. The Oak Ridge Boys

238. The Shirelles

239. Crystal Gayle

240) Who recommended singer Mary Hopkin to Paul McCartney?
   a. Twiggy
   b. Terri Schmidt
   c. Brian Epstein
   d. Phil Collins

241) What city is also known as Music City U.S.A.?

242) Who was the original vocalist for Black Sabbath?

243) He was a member of the Chad Mitchell Trio for almost three years before launching a hugely successful solo career. Name him.

244) What rock singer from east St. Louis was a back-up singer for Ike and Tina Turner and was the first white Ikette?

245) Who is known as the "Man in Black"?

246) What folksinger refused to pay federal income tax because the money would be used for the Victnam War?

247) Who recorded "You Light Up My Life"?

248) Where was Joan Baez born?
   a. San Francisco
   b. Staten Island
   c. Wichita
   d. Houston

. . . Answers

240. a

241. Nashville, Tennessee

242. Ozzy Osbourne

243. John Denver

244. Bonnie Bramlett

245. Johnny Cash

246. Joan Baez

247. Debby Boone

248. b

QUESTIONS

249) Led Zeppelin was the new name for what group?

250) What group recorded the song and elaborate video "Gypsy"?

Match the musical with the film

251) *Applause*   a. *Lili*

252) *Sugar*   b. *Ninotchka*

253) *High Society*   c. *All About Eve*

254) *Silk Stockings* d. *Some Like it Hot*

255) *Carnival*   e. *The Philadelphia Story*

256) What singing group won three Grammy awards as well as fifteen Dove Awards from the Gospel Music Association between 1970 and 1976?

257) Bachman-Turner Overdrive were from what country?

258) The 1955 hit "Rock Around the Clock" was recorded by what group?

259) What group performed "Brain Salad Surgery"?

260) Eric Clapton played guitar, Ginger Baker was on drums, Steve Winwood played the organ, piano and guitar, and sang, and Rick Grech played electric bass and electric violin. What was the name of their group?

. . . Answers

249. The Yardbirds

250. Fleetwood Mac

251. c

252. d

253. e

254. b

255. a

256. The Oak Ridge Boys

257. Canada

258. Bill Haley and the Comets

259. Emerson, Lake and Palmer

260. Blind Faith

261) What female songwriter wrote Kim Carnes' number one hit "Bette Davis Eyes"?

262) Name the female group who recorded "Leader of the Pack" and "I Can Never Go Home Anymore."

263) What is a Stratocaster?

264) Who is Henry John Deutschendorf?

265) What member of the Band starred in the movie of Tom Wolfe's *The Right Stuff*?

266) Their recording of "Sherry" sold 180 thousand copies in one day. The lead singer was known for his high voice. Name the group.

267) The virginal is most closely related to which instrument?
   a. tympani
   b. oboe
   c. recorder
   d. harpsichord

268) Who gave Bob Dylan his start by having him on stage with her when he was still an unknown?

269) *The Hissing of the Summer Lawns* was whose 1977 creation?

. . . *Answers*

261. Jackie DeShannon

262. The Shangri-Las

263. A well-known electric guitar

264. John Denver

265. Levon Helm

266. The Four Seasons

267. d

268. Joan Baez

269. Joni Mitchell

270) What black pop star first recorded "Rambling Rose"?

271) What was the theme song of Count Basie's band?

272) The Fun Boy Three had the 1982 British hit "It Ain't What You Do It's The Way That You Do It" with what female group?

273) What country singer starred in the movie *The Electric Horseman* with Jane Fonda and Robert Redford?

274) Name the Scottish band who did "Pick Up the Pieces."
   a. The Doobie Brothers
   b. Hall and Oates
   c. the Average White Band

275) Her stage name was given to her by her sister who took it from a Southern hamburger chain. Name her.

276) What band's lead singers were later known as the Phlorescent Leech (Flo) and Eddie? "You Baby" was a hit for them in 1966.

277) What singer is known as the "Silver Fox"?

278) Where was *American Bandstand* originally located?

. . . Answers

270. Nat "King" Cole

271. "One O'Clock Jump"

272. Bananarama

273. Willie Nelson

274. c

275. Crystal Gayle

276. The Turtles

277. Charlie Rich

278. Philadelphia

279) What Canadian, a former high school gym teacher, became a regular on a TV show in Canada? Her first album was *What About Me*.

280) What band refused to be photographed when they were not wearing their makeup?

281) In what country did the musical play and film *The Sound of Music* take place?

282) What legendary guitarist played with John Mayall's Bluesbreakers and the Yardbirds?

283) What singer-songwriter wrote "I'm a Believer" and "A Little Bit Me, A Little Bit You" for the Monkees and recorded "Cherry, Cherry" and "Girl, You'll Be a Woman Soon"?

284) What 1960s vocal foursome demonstrated their mastery of counterpoint harmony on such hits as "Monday, Monday" and "I Saw Her Again"?

285) True or false: Bo Diddley's real name was Ellas McDaniel.

286) Besides "Auld Lang Syne" and "For He's a Jolly Good Fellow," what is the most frequently sung song in English?

287) Out of what group did Kenny Rogers help create the First Edition?

. . . Answers

279. Anne Murray

280. Kiss

281. Austria

282. Eric Clapton

283. Neil Diamond

284. The Mamas and the Papas

285. True

286. "Happy Birthday to You"

287. The New Christy Minstrels

288) What is Ringo Starr's original name?

289) The theme song of what famous band was "Moonlight Serenade"?

290) What is the Dutch band that had the successful cuts "Radar Love" and "Twilight Zone"?
   a. Sylvia
   b. the Knack
   c. Smersh
   d. Golden Earring

291) The first guest artist to play at the WSM Barn Dance (which later changed its name to the Grand Ole Opry) on November 28, 1925 was who?

292) Their #1 hit in 1971 was "Horse With No Name" and their hit eleven years later was "You Can Do Magic." What was their name?

293) What Ohio-based group came to prominence with the release of "Beg, Borrow and Steal"?

294) What female vocalist sang "Fame" and "Flashdance . . . What a Feeling"?

295) Who is known for saying "Is everybody happy"?

296) In 1958 what song that sounded like a 33 rpm record played at 45 rpm sold three and a half million copies?

. . . *Answers*

288. Richard Starkey

289. Glenn Miller's

290. d

291. Uncle Jimmy Thompson

292. America

293. The Ohio Express

294. Irene Cara

295. Ted Lewis

296. "The Chipmunk Song"

297) In early 1968 whose song, "The Unicorn," indicated that there was always room for a good Irish song on the charts.

298) Which black vocalist played in the Negro American Baseball League with Memphis and Detroit and eventually made it to the major leagues?

299) What is the name of the supergroup which formed in 1981 with former members of Uriah Heep, Yes, and Emerson, Lake and Palmer?

300) Who is the granddaughter of Red Foley of country music fame?

Match the composer with the musical

301) Richard Rodgers   a. *A Damsel in Distress*

302) Charles Strouse   b. *Allegro*

303) Irving Berlin   c. *Annie*

304) Fredrick Loewe   d. *Annie Get Your Gun*

305) George Gershwin   e. *Camelot*

306) What British band originally had the hit "House of the Rising Sun"?

307) True or false: Head music is music that enhances the marijuana experience.

. . . *Answers*

297. The Irish Rovers

298. Charlie Pride

299. Asia

300. Debby Boone

301. b

302. c

303. d

304. e

305. a

306. The Animals

307. True

308) "Da Doo Ron Ron," "He's a Rebel" and "Then He Kissed Me" were sparkling hits for what female group?

309) True or false: David Seville provided all the Chipmunks' voices.

310) Name Jerry Garcia's long-lived group who had the 1969 palindromic album title *Aoxomoxoa*.

311) What sixties group's lead singer was Joe McDonald, who was best known for his solo performance at Woodstock?

312) What bass guitarist, along with Chick Corea, formed the jazz group Return to Forever?

313) Name the Kinks' first hit single in the United States.

314) Who sent *Greetings From Asbury Park N.J.* in 1973 and performed the 1984 song and video "Atlantic City"?

315) What is acknowledged to have been the first American musical?
  a. *Adonis*
  b. *Wang*
  c. *The Black Crook*

. . . *Answers*

308. The Crystals

309. True

310. Grateful Dead

311. Country Joe and The Fish

312. Stanley Clarke

313. "You Really Got Me"

314. Bruce Springsteen

315. c

QUESTIONS

316) "My Guy" and "Two Lovers" were the work of what Motown singer:
   a. Mary Wells
   b. Martha Reeves
   c. Natalie Cole
   d. Diana Ross

317) Name the Welsh singer who sang the title song on the soundtrack *What's New Pussycat?*

318) Two versions of the song "Breaking Up Is Hard to Do" produced top ten hits for its writer/singer fourteen years apart. Who is he?

319) Her first international hit was "You Don't Have to Say You Love Me" in 1966. She was once England's top female vocalist. Name her.

320) What is the name of the group also known as CSN&Y?

321) True or false: Frank Sinatra sang with Tommy Dorsey's band.

322) What ex-radio announcer sang the 1982 hit "Always on My Mind"?

323) True or false: Cass Elliot sang with the Mugwumps.

. . . Answers

316. a

317. Tom Jones

318. Neil Sedaka

319. Dusty Springfield

320. Crosby, Stills, Nash and Young

321. True

322. Willie Nelson

323. True

QUESTIONS

324) What jazz trumpeter released the successful album *Black Byrd*?

325) "Maybe This Time", "Willkommen" and "Money Money" come from what movie musical?

326) Name the jazz organist who pumped out more than eighty albums on the mighty Hammond organ, including *Walk on the Wild Side* and *Who's Afraid of Virginia Woolf*.

327) What was the name of the record company the Beatles started?

328) What rock singer starred in the film *The Man Who Fell to Earth*?

329) Who recorded the lengthy song "In-A-Gadda-Da-Vida" in 1969?

330) What Canadian teen idol sang "Diana" in 1957?

331) After leaving the Mamas and Papas this entertainer played Las Vegas for one disastrous night. What was her name?

332) Born in Delight, Arkansas, his accomplishments include singing "Wichita Lineman" and acting in the movie *True Grit*. Who is he?

333) Ray Charles, James Brown and Otis Redding all have something in common, besides being successful black singers. What is it?

. . . Answers

324. Donald Byrd

325. *Cabaret*

326. Jimmy Smith

327. Apple

328. David Bowie

329. Iron Butterfly

330. Paul Anka

331. Cass Elliot

332. Glen Campbell

333. All were born in Georgia

334) What rock group had a weekly prime-time television program?

335) This ex-Radcliffe student had a hit in 1977 with a remake of the 1961 "Runaway." Name her.

336) True or false: Ann and Nancy Wilson of the group Heart are twin sisters.

337) What are the names of the three Gibb brothers who formed the Bee Gees?

338) What pop poet performed the albums *The Pretender* and *Running on Empty*?

339) What musician is associated with the tunes "Gone" and "Wings of a Dove"?

340) What soul singer was shot to death by his minister father in 1984?

341) Name one of the only black country music singers to have achieved lasting popularity.

342) Who sang Ashford and Simpson's "Let's Go Get Stoned," making it an international hit?

343) True or false: Berry Gordy worked in an auto plant before he started Motown in 1960.

344) What album has been on the American charts for the greatest length of time (continuously since 1973)?

. . . Answers

334. The Monkees

335. Bonnie Raitt

336. False

337. Barry, Maurice and Robin

338. Jackson Browne

339. Ferlin Husky

340. Marvin Gaye

341. Charlie Pride

342. Ray Charles

343. True

344. Pink Floyd's *The Dark Side of the Moon*

345) What country artist calls his music publishing company Briarpatch Music?

346) According to the 1965 Beatles song, who "doesn't have a point of view, knows not where he's going to"?

347) True or false: Prior to forming the Mothers of Invention, Frank Zappa belonged to Captain Glasspack and The Magic Mufflers.

348) What five-part harmony group had hits in 1966 ("Cherish") and 1967 ("Windy")?

349) Robert Zimmerman recorded and wrote under what name?

350) True or false: The MGs of Booker T. fame chose their name because they were a Memphis group.

Match the song with the musical play

351) "I Don't Know How To Love Him"   a. *South Pacific*

352) "If Ever I Would Leave You"   b. *West Side Story*

353) "People Will Say We're In Love"   c. *Camelot*

354) "One Hand, One Heart"   d. *Jesus Christ Superstar*

355) "Some Enchanted Evening"   e. *Oklahoma*

. . . Answers

345. Eddie Rabbitt

346. "Nowhere Man"

347. False (It's only a legend)

348. The Association

349. Bob Dylan

350. True

351. d

352. c

353. e

354. b

355. a

356) Which female singer was kidnapped from a Nashville shopping center in 1978?

357) Two members of what band were killed in separate motorcycle accidents in 1971 and 1972?
    a. Doobie Brothers
    b. Grateful Dead
    c. Allman Brothers Band
    d. Righteous Brothers

358) What group recorded "Sundays Will Never Be the Same"?

359) "Pop" Staples and his kids, Pervis, Cleotha and Mavis, had a 1971 hit, "Respect Yourself," under what name?

360) What male singer boasts a travelling medicine man for a grandfather?

361) Dave Clark of the Dave Clark Five played what instrument?

362) What do these two stage musicals, *Half a Sixpence* and *The Boy Friend* have in common?
    a. the musical scores were written by the same man
    b. both played in the same theatre in New York
    c. both were made into a film at some point

. . . *Answers*

356. Tammy Wynette

357. c

358. Spanky and Our Gang

359. The Staple Singers

360. Marty Robbins

361. Drums

362. c

363) "Wah-Watusi" was the claim to fame for what silk-substitute group?

364) Who joined Motown records as a secretary and later recorded "Dancing in the Streets," "Jimmy Mack" and "Honey Chile" with the Vandellas?

365) Chrissie Hynde is the lead singer for what group?

366) True or false: The Oak Ridge Boys were initially rock singers.

367) What Indian musician is responsible for making the sitar a well-known instrument in the U.S.?

368) Helen O'Connell sang for what big band?

369) Name Procol Harum's 1967 hit featuring a cantata-like organ.

370) Name the person who wrote the musical scores for the films and specials *White Christmas*, *Holiday Inn* and *Top Hat*?

371) How many Brandenburg Concertos did Bach write?

372) Who was the first female to be named Entertainer of the Year by the Country Music Association?

. . . *Answers*

363. The Orlons

364. Martha Reeves

365. The Pretenders

366. False

367. Ravi Shankar

368. Jimmy Dorsey's

369. "A Whiter Shade Of Pale"

370. Irving Berlin

371. Six

372. Loretta Lynn

373) Quincy Jones was the producer for which teenage girl singer who whimpered "It's My Party"?

374) At forty-two years of age in 1961 who recorded "Sixteen Tons"?

375) "Here Comes the Sun," a hit for Richie Havens, is a song from which Beatles album?

376) In which year did the Supremes record "Love is like an Itching in My Heart"?
    a. 1961
    b. 1962
    c. 1964

377) What group from the fifties recorded the hits "Only You," "The Great Pretender" and "My Prayer"?

378) "Don't Rain on My Parade" came from what musical play?

379) What group could "teach your children well"?

380) Who first appeared on the charts with "The Universal Soldier"?

381) Who was Joan Baez's singing partner in the 1965 hit "There But for Fortune"?
    a. Phil Ochs   c. Manfred Mann
    b. Bob Dylan   d. George Sheats

. . . Answers

373. Lesley Gore

374. Tennessee Ernie Ford

375. *Abbey Road*

376. b

377. The Platters

378. *Funny Girl*

379. Crosby, Stills, Nash and Young

380. Glen Campbell

381. a

382) What English group's first major hit in the U.S. was "Look Through Any Window"?

383) What is jazz pianist Earl Hines' nickname?

384) What was the Beatles' first hit in America? It was #1 for seven weeks in 1964.

385) What is Boy George's real name?

386) In 1968 they released *Anthem of the Sun*.

387) The eerie, wavering music accompanying early horror movies was produced by what electronic, hand-controlled instrument?

388) He became well-known for his recording of "Lonely Teardrops." He started in Detroit as the lead singer of the Dominoes. Who is he?

389) *Yessongs* was the 1973 three-record release of what group?

390) "Walk Away Renee" and "Pretty Ballerina" were recorded by what group?

391) True or false: Frank Beard of ZZ Top is one of the distinctively bearded members of the group.

. . . *Answers*

382. The Hollies

383. Fatha

384. "I Want to Hold Your Hand"

385. George O'Dowd

386. Grateful Dead

387. Theremin

388. Jackie Wilson

389. Yes

390. The Left Banke

391. False (His beard is short and unlike the trademark beard of his group.)

392) What group, specializing in satire and sophisticated comedy, included Paul McCartney's brother, Mike McGear?

393) Jazz, Precision and Musicmaster are electric basses from what company?
   a. Harmony
   b. Fender
   c. Gibson
   d. Gretch

394) Whose band was called the Buckaroos?

395) What Canadian singer/composer wrote the 1969 hit "Both Sides Now" and in 1982 recorded the album *Wild Things Run Fast*?

396) In 1965 Barry McGuire became famous for singing what protest song?

397) Who created "Theme From Rocky XIII" and the Michael Jackson parody "Eat It"?

398) Who led the Royal Canadians?

399) Bobby Hebb's successful single was
   a. "Somewhere Tonite"
   b. "Sunny"
   c. "Release Me"
   d. "What It Takes"

. . . Answers

392. Scaffold

393. b

394. Buck Owens

395. Joni Mitchell

396. "Eve of Destruction"

397. "Weird" Al Yankovic

398. Guy Lombardo

399. b

400) Name the four country stars who recorded *Outlaws*.

Match the singer with the hit

401) "Rocky Mountain High"   a. Willie Nelson

402) "On the Road Again"   b. John Denver

403) "Ladies Love Outlaws"   c. Kenny Rogers

404) "The Gambler"   d. Waylon Jennings

405) "Song Sung Blue"   e. Neil Diamond

406) Guitarists Eric Clapton, Jeff Beck and Jimmy Page all played with what British group?

407) What bubblegum group was known for singles, "Simon Says" and "1, 2, 3 Red Light"?

408) The J. Geils Band changed its name for one album, *Monkey Island*, and then changed it back. What was their temporary name?

409) He had two shows on Broadway in the 1960–61 season, *The Unsinkable Molly Brown* and *The Music Man*. What was his name?

... *Answers*

400. Waylon Jennings, Jessie Colter, Willie Nelson and Tompall Glaser

401. b

402. a

403. d

404. c

405. e

406. The Yardbirds

407. 1910 Fruitgum Company

408. Geils

409. Meredith Willson

QUESTIONS

410) Igor Stravinsky's opera *The Rake's Progress* was based on what artist's pictures?
   a. Picasso
   b. Dali
   c. Manet
   d. Hogarth

411) Who started the Coral Reefer Band?

412) What Detroit singer knows that "Rock and Roll Never Forgets"?

413) What was the name of the small town in which *The Music Man* took place?

414) Who was responsible for establishing the guitar as a respectable concert instrument?

415) Name the Canadian group that were sometimes considered imitations of the Vanilla Fudge.

416) What genuine sister group from California recorded "Yes We Can Can" and "He's So Shy"?

417) What team of musical score writers wrote *The King and I*, *South Pacific* and *Oklahoma*?

418) What Russian composer died in 1953, on the same day as Stalin?

. . . Answers

410. d

411. Jimmy Buffett

412. Bob Seger

413. River City

414. Andres Segovia

415. Rotary Connection

416. The Pointer Sisters

417. Richard Rodgers and Oscar Hammerstein II

418. Sergei Prokofiev

419) The songs "Sunrise Sunset" and "If I Were a Rich Man" came from what musical play?

420) What blind Puerto Rican sang the hit "Light My Fire" in 1968?

421) Which musical play ran the shortest time on the stage?
   a. *Kiss Me Kate*
   b. *The Wiz*
   c. *Damn Yankees*

422) "Judy's Turn to Cry" was the sequel to which of Lesley Gore's hits?

423) True or false: The Beach Boys' Mike Love is Brian Wilson's cousin.

424) True or false: Adolphe Sax invented the saxophone in 1840.

425) In what year did Otis Redding's fatal plane crash happen?

426) In 1972, who nearly drove his pappy to drinking by driving his hot rod Lincoln?

427) Who was the first country artist elected into the Hall of Fame while still alive?

. . . Answers

419. *Fiddler on the Roof*

420. Jose Feliciano

421. b

422. "It's My Party"

423. True

424. True

425. 1967

426. Commander Cody and His Lost Planet Airmen

427. Roy Acuff

428) What four sisters from Oakland started singing in the church where their parents were preachers?

429) Name a country artist who was also an athlete, helicopter pilot, paratrooper and janitor.

430) Janis Joplin sang with what group?

431) What male vocalist has overcome his blindness to become a big country star?

432) What country music guitarist became vice president of RCA in 1968?

433) In 1967 what group came to national attention with the release of "Apples, Peaches, Pumpkin Pie"?

434) What "cult" group recorded "Transmaniacon MC" and "Cities on Flame With Rock and Roll"?

435) True or false: Englebert Humperdinck's real name is Gerry Dorsey.

436) Name the vocalist who had the 1979 #1 hit "No More Tears (Enough Is Enough)" with Barbra Streisand and the 1983 hit "She Works Hard for the Money."

437) She was the Queen of the Blues in the forties. Her death in 1959 shocked the music industry. Name her.

. . . *Answers*

428. The Pointer Sisters

429. Kris Kristofferson

430. Big Brother and the Holding Company

431. Ronnie Milsap

432. Chet Atkins

433. Jay and the Techniques

434. Blue Oyster Cult

435. True

436. Donna Summer

437. Billie Holiday

438) True or false: Liberace took piano lessons from Paderewski.

439) True or false: Bubblegum music, such as "Chewy Chewy" and "Yummy Yummy Yummy" was popular in 1968.

440) *Born to Boogie* is a documentary made in 1973 by Ringo Starr about what group?

441) In 1959 whose hit "Tom Dooley" rose to #1 on the charts?

442) Name the Australian singer who did the song and video "Affair of the Heart" in which his memories return in a mini-movie.

443) Who did the original versions of "Ain't Too Proud to Beg" and "Just My Imagination (Running Away With Me)," both of which were later recorded by the Rolling Stones?

444) What former physics student has a well-known synthesizer as his namesake?

445) What country singer had a job with a radio station in Lubbock, Texas in 1950 at the age of twelve?

446) James Osterberg changed his name to Iggy Pop after going by what other name for a few years?

. . . Answers

438. True

439. True

440. T-Rex

441. The Kingston Trio

442. Rick Springfield

443. The Temptations

444. Robert Moog

445. Waylon Jennings

446. Iggy Stooge

447) Who recorded "The Devil Went Down to Georgia"?

448) What group recorded *The Basement Tapes* with Bob Dylan in 1966 while he was recovering from a motorcycle accident?

449) True or false: Olivia Newton-John was born in Australia.

450) Agnetha, Bjorn, Benny and Anni-Frid comprise what acronymically-named group?

Match the composer with the musical

451) Jerome Kern   a. *Peter Pan*

452) Mitch Leigh   b. *Man of La Mancha*

453) Leonard Bernstein   c. *Seesaw*

454) Cy Coleman   d. *Night Boat*

455) Cole Porter   e. *Silk Stockings*

456) Phil Silvers and Nancy Walker were in what play together in 1960? What was its name?

457) What former teacher sang the #1 hit in 1972 "The First Time Ever I Saw Your Face"?

. . . *Answers*

447. The Charlie Daniels Band

448. The Band

449. False (England)

450. Abba

451. d

452. b

453. a

454. c

455. e

456. *Do-Re-Mi*

457. Roberta Flack

58) Rudy Vallee played J.B. Biggley in what musical play?

59) The Bach unaccompanied cello suites were unknown until they were performed by what master of the violoncello?

60) Which entertainer was known as "The Cherokee Cowboy"?

61) What vocal duo wrote the Motown classics "Ain't No Mountain High Enough" and "Ain't Nothing Like the Real Thing"?

62) He sang "Splish Splash" and also wrote it. He won Grammy awards for Best New Singer and Record of the Year in 1959. Name him.

63) What English rock star played the role of John Merrick in the Broadway play *The Elephant Man*?

64) "Winchester Cathedral" was originally recorded by what group?

65) What former Genesis vocalist created the successful single accompanying video "Shock the Monkey"?

66) Which country star started an International Foundation for the Prevention of Child Abuse?

. . . Answers

467) Who was the early rock great that lost popularity for marrying his thirteen-year-old cousin?

468) What relation were Carl and Pearl Butler to each other?

469) The 1948 introduction of what recording medium by Columbia Records produced a radical change in the recording industry?

470) These brother songwriters were initially under contract to Disney. They wrote songs for such films as *Chitty Chitty Bang Bang*, *Jungle Book* and *Mary Poppins*. Who are they?

471) Who is called Soul Sister Number One?

472) The musical play *How to Succeed in Business Without Really Trying* opened in what year?

473) *Themes and Variations* is the title of the autobiography of what German conductor?

474) They were originally known as the Robins. They hit #1 with "Yakety Yak" in 1958 under what name?

475) The Wilson brothers, Brian, Dennis, and Carl, were members of what band?

. . . Answers

467. Jerry Lee Lewis

468. Husband and wife

469. The twelve-inch LP record

470. Richard and Robert Sherman

471. Aretha Franklin

472. 1961

473. Bruno Walter

474. The Coasters

475. The Beach Boys

476) Who was nominated for Country Music Association Female Vocalist of the Year four times from 1975 to 1978 and lost each time?

477) Frankie Avalon appeared in what 1978 film?

478) When the Rolling Stones' rhythm guitarist Brian Jones left the group in 1969, who replaced him?

479) Who has been called the Latin voice of rock and is the leader of the band with albums *Santana* and *Caravanserai*?

480) Who is known for playing Champagne Music?

481) Who wrote the Beatles' "Roll Over Beethoven" and "Rock and Roll Music"?

482) Gertrude Lawrence was starring in a musical play when she died after eighteen months of the play's run. What play was she starring in?

483) What easygoing California outlaw group recorded "Desperado" and "One of These Nights"?

484) Who was married to Merle Haggard in the early days of their careers and accompanied him to San Quentin where she cut her own album of mostly prison songs?

485) What was Janis Joplin's nickname?

. . . *Answers*

476. Barbara Mandrell

477. *Grease*

478. Mick Taylor

479. Carlos Santana

480. Lawrence Welk

481. Chuck Berry

482. *The King and I*

483. The Eagles

484. Leona Williams

485. Pearl

486) What country band was invited to perform at former President Jimmy Carter's Inaugural Ball, as well as at the White House?

487) What West Indian female vocalist did "Me, Myself, I", "Love and Affection" and "Show Some Emotion"?

488) What 1920s musical family were Alvin Pleasant, Sara and Maybelle part of?

489) Name the soul artist who appeared at the Monterey Pop Festival in 1967 and who had the hit "(Sittin' on) The Dock of the Bay."

490) These two men had two shows playing on Broadway in 1960–61 season, *My Fair Lady* and *Camelot*.

491) Moussorgsky's *Pictures at an Exhibition* was recorded by what popular rock group in 1971?

492) Who wrote the hit "The Twist"?
   a. Hank Ballard
   b. Chubby Checker
   c. Chuck Berry

493) A totally silent work titled "4' 33" " (Four minutes, thirty-three seconds) was composed by what twentieth century experimentalist?

494) In what year did Eddie Cochran record "Summertime Blues"?

. . . Answers

486. The Charlie Daniels Band

487. Joan Armatrading

488. The Carter Family

489. Otis Redding

490. Alan Jay Lerner and Frederick Loewe

491. Emerson, Lake and Palmer

492. a

493. John Cage

494. 1958

495) This singer recorded his first album at the age of eighteen. His middle and last names are Rogers Nelson. Name him.

496) Who preceded Dolly Parton on Porter Wagoner's show in the mid-sixties?

497) What legendary rock performer played the psychedelic guitar with his teeth and behind his back, and set it on fire at the 1967 Monterey Pop Festival?

498) Bobby Rydell was in a rock 'n' roll combo called Rocco and the Saints. Who was also part of this group?
   a. Frankie Avalon
   b. Bobby Darin
   c. Fabian

499) Connie Stevens and Edd Byrnes had what fifties top twenty hit?

500) Who wrote "You Are My Sunshine"?

Great Diminutives: Match the artist with the song

501) Little Anthony and the Imperials   a. "Good Golly, Miss Molly"

502) Little Richard   b. "Fingertips (Part 2)"

503) Little Stevie Wonder   c. "Tears on My Pillow"

. . . Answers

495. Prince

496. Norma Jean Beasler

497. Jimi Hendrix

498. a

499. "Kookie, Kookie (Lend Me Your Comb)"

500. Jimmie Davis

501. c

502. a

503. b

QUESTIONS

504) John Stewart, who wrote the Monkees' "Daydream Believer," used to belong to what folk group?

505) What instrument is Gerry Mulligan known for?

506) John Fred and the Playboy Band had what single hit in 1967?
   a. "Lucy in the Sky With Diamonds"
   b. "Judy in Disguise (With Glasses)"
   c. "Jamie Lee in Playboy Heaven"

507) The Metropolis Blue Quartet spun off what group:
   a. the Four Seasons
   b. the Mamas and the Papas
   c. the Yardbirds

508) The "New World" Symphony is whose Symphony No. 9 in E-minor?

509) What male singer collaborated with Nancy Sinatra on "Jackson"?

510) What famous American composer wrote the scores for *Peter Gunn, Charade*, and *The Pink Panther*?

511) Who released the rock classic "Great Balls of Fire" in 1957?

512) What English group recorded the 1969 album *In the Court of the Crimson King*?

. . . *Answers*

504. The Kingston Trio

505. Baritone sax

506. b

507. c

508. Dvorak

509. Lee Hazlewood

510. Henry Mancini

511. Jerry Lee Lewis

512. King Crimson

513) Who, at the age of 16, recorded "Society's Child" in 1967?

514) What ex-member of the Herd and Humble Pie "came alive" in 1975?

515) What singer was selected for a Grammy as the Most Promising Male Vocalist in 1962 and 1963?

516) Who was the Beatles' record producer?

517) James Barry Keefer recorded "98.6" under what name?

518) What group did the song and video "Burning Down the House," an anti-suburban theme?
   a. the Damned
   b. U2
   c. Talking Heads
   d. the Tubes

519) Who recorded the hit single "Love is the Drug" in 1975?

520) Who became Motown's star of the screen with *Lady Sings the Blues, Mahogany*, and *The Wiz*?

521) In 1968 what group had a starring role in the film *Paint Your Wagon*?

. . . Answers

513. Janis Ian

514. Peter Frampton

515. Jack Jones

516. George Martin

517. Keith

518. c

519. Roxy Music

520. Diana Ross

521. The Nitty Gritty Dirt Band

522) What American group recorded "Rock This Town" and "Stray Cat Strut"?

523) Who became a country music star without an agent or a manager (he handled both jobs)? His best known song was "Slippin' Around."

524) What Brazilian keyboard player had a hit in 1973 with his interpretation of "Also Sprach Zarathustra (2001)"?
   a. Deodato
   b. Sergio Mendes
   c. Flora Purim

525) This blind singer/guitarist sang a controversial rendition of "The Star Spangled Banner" during the 1968 World Series. Name him.

526) "Betcha By Golly, Wow" and "You Make Me Feel Brand New" were the stylish smash hits of what group?

527) What old-time country singer hails from Nova Scotia?

528) Which Rolling Stone died in the late 1960s?

529) Three of the Starlighters (Joey Dee's back-up group) went on to form what rock group?

530) What American female singer recorded "Gloria" in 1983 and "Self Control" in 1984?

. . . Answers

531) True or false: The Soul Survivors were all black musicians.

532) Siouxsie Sioux of the Banshees teamed up with Budgie from the Slits to form what band in 1982?

533) Who was the lead singer of the Seeds?
   a. Sky Saxon
   b. Tim Bogert
   c. Jean Hartnett

534) *Sweet Baby James* and *Mud Slide Slim and the Blue Horizon* were two of what composer/guitarist's successful albums?

535) In the big band era, who was the Hi-De-Ho Man?

536) In the year 1969 Zager and Evans created what futuristic hit?

537) Who recorded the best-selling record "Roses are Red"?

538) What poet-novelist wrote "Suzanne"?

539) "Joshua" was her first #1 single. She wrote such songs as "Coat of Many Colors," "My Tennessee Mountain Home" and "Love Is Like a Butterfly." What is her name?

. . . Answers

531. False

532. The Creatures

533. a

534. James Taylor

535. Cab Calloway

536. "In the Year 2525"

537. Bobby Vinton

538. Leonard Cohen

539. Dolly Parton

QUESTIONS

540) Dr. Hook's hit song, "The Cover of the Rolling Stone" was written by what Playboy cartoonist?
    a. Gahan Wilson
    b. Sadi
    c. Shel Silverstein
    d. Mort Walker

541) What black singer not only sang the lead in his single "I Believe to My Soul" but also dubbed in the four falsetto girls' parts in the background?

542) What trio had the hit "Marrakesh Express"?

543) Who starred in the movie *The Best Little Whorehouse in Texas* with Burt Reynolds?

544) What trumpeter established his unique "Ameriachi" sound in 1962 with "The Lonely Bull"?

545) This Mexican-American from Texas was billed in 1972 as "the Next Big Thing." He had sex appeal but hasn't made it any bigger than "Ridin' My Thumb to Mexico" and "That's the Way Love Does." Name him.

546) "That'll Be the Day" and "Peggy Sue" were hits by what performer known for his horn-rimmed glasses?

547) What group, besides recording on their own, played back-up for a number of the Stax-Volt artists, such as Sam and Dave, Wilson Pickett, and Otis Redding? Their first album, recorded in 1962, was *Green Onions*.

. . . *Answers*

540. c

541. Ray Charles

542. Crosby, Stills and Nash

543. Dolly Parton

544. Herb Alpert

545. Johnny Rodriguez

546. Buddy Holly

547. Booker T. and the MGs

548) What brother-sister team ended when one of them died of anorexia?

549) What Hank Ballard tune made Chubby Checker a star in 1960?

550) Ex-window dresser Boy George now sings for what group?

Match each stage name with the artist's original name

551) Stevie Wonder	a.	Don Van Vliet
552) Captain Beefheart	b.	Annie Mae Bullock
553) Tina Turner	c.	Steveland Judkins
554) Mama Cass Elliot	d.	Reginald Dwight
555) Elton John	e.	Ernest Evans
556) Chubby Checker	f.	Naomi Cohen

557) In 1978, this group from Akron, Ohio asked "Are we not men?" Who are they?

558) Who was put on the Group W bench for littering?

559) What pair once recorded under the name Caesar and Cleo?

560) Who formed the group Utopia?

. . . *Answers*

548. The Carpenters

549. "The Twist"

550. Culture Club

551. c

552. a

553. b

554. f

555. d

556. e

557. Devo

558. Arlo Guthrie

559. Sonny and Cher

560. Todd Rundgren

QUESTIONS

561) Which play was awarded the Pulitzer Prize for Drama?
    a. *South Pacific*
    b. *My Fair Lady*
    c. *No, No, Nanette*

562) Who won four Grammy Awards in 1971 for her album *Tapestry*?

563) What singer replaced Signe Anderson in the Jefferson Airplane?

564) The Isley Brothers had a 1974 hit with "Summer Breeze" which was a gold record original of what duo?

565) "Tutti Frutti" and "Long Tall Sally" were first recorded by what artist?

566) How many grooves are there in a standard 33 1/3rpm record?

567) Who wrote "I Can't Stop Loving You," "Sweet Dreams" and "Oh Lonesome Me"?

568) "People Are Strange" and "Hello, I Love You" were hits for what group?

569) "On the Road Again" was from an original musical score by Willie Nelson for what film?

. . . Answers

561. a

562. Carole King

563. Grace Slick

564. Seals and Crofts

565. Little Richard

566. One

567. Don Gibson

568. The Doors

569. *Honeysuckle Rose*

570) What British rock "orchestra" did "Can't Get It Out of My Head" in 1975 and "Don't Bring Me Down" in 1979?

571) Their hit "I Heard It Through the Grapevine" sold two million copies. Name the group.

572) Name the group that featured Martha Davis' deep voice on the 1982 hit "Only the Lonely" and the 1984 success "Suddenly Last Summer."

573) Ian Whitcomb has written numerous books about the history of popular music. What was his top ten hit of 1965?

574) What British vocalist topped the charts with "Downtown"?

575) What artist put four records in the top ten simultaneously: "I Want To Be With You Always," "Always Late," "Mom and Dad's Waltz" and "Travelin' Blues"?

576) What former boxer and construction worker wrote and sang the hits "I'm a Man" in 1955 and "Say Man" in 1959?

577) In his single "San Francisco," who reminded us to wear flowers in our hair?

. . . *Answers*

570. Electric Light Orchestra

571. Gladys Knight and the Pips

572. The Motels

573. "You Turn Me On"

574. Petula Clark

575. Lefty Frizzell

576. Bo Diddley

577. Scott McKenzie

578) Before her sex change operation, (s)he created the successful synthesized album *Switched On Bach*. What was his name?

579) What sixties group recorded "I Had Too Much to Dream Last Night"?

580) Who is the "space cowboy" that is "living in the USA"?

581) Who wrote "Harper Valley PTA"?

582) What was John Lennon's first wife's name?

583) True or false: *The Little Tycoon* was the first musical on Broadway.

584) True or false: A properly trained human voice has been able to cover the musical range of the piano.

585) True or false: The Nazz featured Todd Rundgren on guitar.

586) Name the renowned jazz bassist whose album *Journey to Love* fetaures a Jeff Beck solo on the title cut.

587) Name the Australian group who recorded "Georgy Girl" for the film of the same name in 1966.

. . . Answers

578. Walter Carlos

579. The Electric Prunes

580. Steve Miller

581. Tom T. Hall

582. Cynthia

583. False

584. True

585. True

586. Stanley Clarke

587. The Seekers

588) Originally founded in the 1600s in Constantinople, Turkey, the Zildjian company is known for what musical product?

589) What two artists first called themselves Tom and Jerry in the late fifties?

590) Randy Crawford lept to stardom when she recorded the 1979 hit "Street Life" with what virtuoso jazz group?

591) In what year did Paul Anka record his first number one hit, "Diana"?

592) Joe Cocker sang the hit song "Up Where We Belong" with what female singer?

593) Who was the original Higgins in *My Fair Lady* on Broadway in 1956?

594) In 1958, who became the first American pianist to win the Tschaikovsky Competition in Moscow?

595) Who was known as "the King of Rock 'n' Roll"?

596) Who was named Rock 'n' Roll Pop Star for 1972 by *Rolling Stone* magazine and received a Grammy nomination for "Call Me"?
    a. Marvin Gaye
    b. Al Green
    c. Laura Branigan
    d. Larry Schmidt

. . . Answers

588. Cymbals

589. Simon and Garfunkel

590. The Crusaders

591. 1958

592. Jennifer Warnes

593. Rex Harrison

594. Van Cliburn

595. Elvis Presley

596. b

597) What group's original name was the Quarrymen?
   a. the Dave Clark Five
   b. the Yardbirds
   c. the Beatles

598) "Jenny Take a Ride" was a hit in the sixties for what Detroit group?

599) Who is Harold Lloyd Jenkins?

600) What group hears "the low spark of high-heeled boys"?

Match the musician with his instrument

601) Miles Davis	a. Bass
602) Lionel Hampton	b. Piano
603) Keith Jarrett	c. Trumpet
604) Lenny White	d. Fluegelhorn
605) Ron Carter	e. Drums
606) Chuck Mangione	f. Vibes

607) The musical play *Coco* brought what "superstar" actress back to the stage for her first musical?

. . . *Answers*

597. c

598. Mitch Ryder and the Detroit Wheels

599. Conway Twitty

600. Traffic

601. c

602. f

603. b

604. e

605. a

606. d

607. Katherine Hepburn

608) In 1984 what German group did "Rock You Like a Hurricane"?

    a. Nena
    b. Trio
    c. The Scorpions
    d. Kraftwerk

609) What actor played the part of Horace Vandergelder in the 1968 film version of *Hello Dolly?*

610) Name the musical form, generally improvised, which has a name derived from the Creole word for coition.

611) With three instrumentalists he formed the Hoboken Four and won first prize on "The Major Bowes Original Amateur Hour." Name him.

612) Donny is the name of the youngest member of what successful family vocal act?

613) Who is Roy Clark's co-host on the country TV show *Hee-Haw?*

614) The 1982 *Winds of Change* album was done by what group that has been together for twenty years?

615) What female group toured with the Beatles in 1966?

. . . *Answers*

608. c

609. Walter Matthau

610. Jazz

611. Frank Sinatra

612. The Osmonds

613. Buck Owens

614. Jefferson Starship

615. The Ronettes

616) Who had 1984 success with "Girls Just Want to Have Fun"?

617) What country singer is a former professional boxer?

618) Who was the drummer for Cream and Air Force?

619) This group was originally known as the Rhondells. In 1966 they released their biggest single album, "Red Rubber Ball." Who are they?

620) What British band chose their name from the villian in the movie *Barbarella* which starred Jane Fonda?

621) Who starred in the title role in the musical play *You're a Good Man, Charlie Brown*?

622) What brother duo whose hits include "Wake Up Little Susie" and "Bird Dog" had a 1984 comeback concert in London?

623) What entertainer owns the largest nightclub in the world, a place near Houston named after him?

624) True or false: Ike Turner adapted his wife Tina's image from the comic book heroine of the 1950s, Sheena, Queen of the Jungle.

. . . Ánswers

616. Cyndi Lauper

617. Roy Clark

618. Ginger Baker

619. The Cyrkle

620. Duran Duran

621. Gary Burghoff

622. The Everly Brothers

623. Mickey Gilley

624. True

625) She was thirteen years old in 1972. She recorded such tunes as "Delta Dawn" and "Would You Lay With Me." Who is she?

626) Gordon Sumner of the Police is better known by what nickname?

627) Name the award given by the National Academy of the Recording Arts and Sciences for achievements in phonograph recordings.

628) What is the better-known name of Pat Andrejewski?

629) Name the David Seville hit which ended with "Walla walla bing bang."

630) Which notable American composer attended the Harvard Law School and later joined the French Foreign Legion?

631) What group first recorded "Wipe Out"?
   a. the Beach Boys
   b. the Surfaris
   c. Jan and Dean

632) This jazz keyboard superstar's video includes dangling, robotic legs kicking to the beat of "Autodrive." Name him.

. . . *Answers*

625. Tanya Tucker

626. Sting

627. Grammy

628. Pat Benatar

629. "Witch Doctor"

630. Cole Porter

631. b

632. Herbie Hancock

633) What instrument did Bunny Berigan play?

634) What British singer and friend of the Beatles did the song "You're My World"?

635) He wrote his first song, "Standing in the Shadows," in 1966. His father was a well-known country songwriter and singer who died when his son was only three years old. Name the son.

636) What high camp style singer had a hit with "Do You Wanna Dance"?

637) What rockabilly singer wrote and first recorded "Blue Suede Shoes"?

638) Who wrote "Empty Garden," the 1982 tribute to John Lennon?

639) What group recorded "Time Has Come Today"?

640) What singer-songwriter, later killed in an airplane crash, wrote "I Got a Name" and "Time in a Bottle"?

641) In what play did Lena Horne and Ricardo Montalban head the cast?

642) Frankie Valli was the lead singer for what group with the hits "Let's Hang On" and "I've Got You Under My Skin"?

. . . Answers

633. Trumpet

634. Cilla Black

635. Hank Williams, Jr.

636. Bette Midler

637. Carl Perkins

638. Elton John

639. The Chambers Brothers

640. Jim Croce

641. *Jamaica*

642. The Four Seasons

643) Name the songwriter known as Whispering Bill who wrote such tunes as "City Lights" and "Po' Folks."

644) True or false: Phil Spector produced *A Christmas Gift to You* in 1963.

645) Gershwin, Berlin and others regarded this man as the greatest composer of all. He worked with Oscar Hammerstein on *Showboat*. Some of his other works include: *Can't Help Singing, The Cat and the Fiddle* and *Three Sisters*. Name him.

646) What type of saxophone is between the soprano and tenor saxes in size and pitch?

647) Who has a lifetime contract as the Coca-Cola ambassadoress?

648) "Dancing Queen," an American #1 hit in 1977, was done by what European group?

649) He was a boy actor, film director, a casting director at CBS and then a television producer. He was also a composer and lyricist of the Broadway plays *Funny Girl, Carnival* and *Sugar*. Name him.

650) Who is known for his bent trumpet?

. . . *Answers*

643. Bill Anderson

644. True

645. Jerome Kern

646. Alto saxophone

647. Dottie West

648. Abba

649. Robert Merrill

650. Dizzy Gillespie

Match the Beatle song with the year of its release

551)	1962	a.	"A Hard Day's Night"
552)	1964	b.	"Yellow Submarine"
553)	1965	c.	"Hello Goodbye"
554)	1966	d.	"Hey Jude"
555)	1967	e.	"Help!"
556)	1968	f.	"Love Me Do"

657) True or false: Audrey Hepburn did not sing the songs in the motion picture *My Fair Lady*.

658) *Johnny's Greatest Hits* was on *Billboard's* best-seller chart for 490 consecutive weeks. Who is Johnny?

659) Which of these albums was the top-selling in 1967?
    a. *Dr. Zhivago*
    b. *The Doors*
    c. *S.R.O.*

660) What popular British group is "Hungry Like a Wolf"?

661) True or false: All three of the original Supremes were born and raised in Detroit.

. . . Answers

651. f

652. a

653. e

654. b

655. c

656. d

657. True

658. Johnny Mathis

659. a

660. Duran Duran

661. False

562) True or false: Pink Floyd took their name from Georgia bluesmen Pink Anderson and Floyd Council.

563) In 1965 who released their first album *Do You Believe in Magic?*

564) "A Well Respected Man" and "Lola" were two of the more successful cuts from what British group?

565) Who recorded and won a Grammy for the hit "Happiest Girl in the Whole U.S.A."?

566) True or false: The choice of the Beatles' name was influenced by Buddy Holly's Crickets.

567) Who is Loretta Lynn's younger sister?

568) What was the earliest all-female rock group signed to a major recording label?

569) What female English singer has appeared in twenty-five movies and recorded her first single at the age of sixteen? In 1965 she recorded her hit "I Know a Place."

570) Who sang "Arthur's Theme" from the Dudley Moore movie *Arthur?*

571) Known as "Lady Soul," the singer burst onto the music scene in 1967 with her hit, "Respect."

. . . *Answers*

662. True

663. The Lovin' Spoonful

664. The Kinks

665. Donna Fargo

666. True

667. Crystal Gayle

668. Goldie and the Gingerbreads

669. Petula Clark

670. Christopher Cross

671. Aretha Franklin

672) What do you call an eighth note?
   a. quaver
   b. semiquaver
   c. demisemiquaver
   d. hemidemisemiquaver

673) Which of the following was not sung in the Broadway musical hit *Funny Girl*?
   a. "People"
   b. "Sadie Sadie"
   c. "My Man"

674) What guitarist created a successful album named after the Beatles' "A Day in the Life"?

675) Who recorded "Garden Party"?

676) Who sang the hits "Itsy Bitsy Teenie Weenie Yellow Polka Dot Bikini" and "Sealed With a Kiss"?

677) What British trio of the late 1960s recorded the albums *Wheels of Fire* and *Disraeli Gears*?

678) Who sang the #1 song in 1978, "Too Much Too Little Too Late"
   a. Mama Cass
   b. Johnny Mathis
   c. Barbra Streisand
   d. Captain Sensible

... *Answers*

672. a

673. c

674. Wes Montgomery

675. Rick Nelson

676. Brian Hyland

677. Cream

678. b

679) What musical was made into a film in the mid-seventies starring John Travolta and Olivia Newton-John?

680) Chubby Checker, Charlie Parker and Bessie Smith all came from what city?

681) Who wrote "Folsom Prison Blues"?

682) What British singer did the vocals for the group War?
    a. Eric Burdon
    b. David Bowie
    c. Iggy Pop
    d. James Burton

683) The musical play *Camelot* was adapted from what book?

684) What Scottish singer sang the theme to the James Bond movie *For Your Eyes Only*?

685) What do "Don't Be Cruel" and "Jailhouse Rock" have in common?
    a. Both were written by the same person
    b. Both were #1 on Popular, Rhythm & Blues and Country charts
    c. Both were recorded in the same year

686) What all-female group of the early seventies recorded *Charity Ball* in 1971?

. . . Answers

679. *Grease*

680. Philadelphia

681. Johnny Cash

682. a

683. *The Once and Future King*

684. Sheena Easton

685. b

686. Fanny

687) True or false: The musical play *Fanny* was about Fanny Brice.

688) Name the creator of *Tumbleweed Connection* who was known for his wild sunglasses and high-soled shoes.

689) This singer-songwriter was also a journalist and a sailor. He wrote of pirates, smuggling, Southern people and places. A few of his songs were "Woman Goin' Crazy on Caroline Street" and "Kick It In, Second Wind." Name him.

690) Playwright Sam Shepard was once the drummer of what band whose "If You Want to Be a Bird" is featured on the soundtrack to *Easy Rider*?

691) True or false: Phil Everly is the older of the Everly Brothers.

692) Who wrote the Monkees' "Take a Giant Step" and Aretha Franklin's "You Make Me Feel Like A Natural Woman"?

693) Who was the country musician that signed to perform with the Imperials for a Las Vegas gig?

694) Nico was a lead singer for what bizarre, mixed media troupe organized by Andy Warhol in 1967?

695) What instrument is over four feet long and is the most popular stringed instrument in India?

. . . *Answers*

687. False

688. Elton John

689. Jimmy Buffett

690. The Holy Medal Rounders

691. False

692. Carole King and Gerry Coffin

693. Larry Gatlin

694. The Velvet Underground

695. Sitar

696) What is the full name of the group ELO?

697) Richard Penniman sang under what name?

698) Who used the phrase "Excuse me while I kiss the sky"?

699) What group recorded their first big single, "The Letter," in 1967?
   a. the Righteous Brothers
   b. the Box Tops
   c. the Association

700) What progressive jazz trumpeter created *Bitches Brew*?

Match these songs with the movies they are from

701) "The Entertainer" (Scott Joplin)   a. *Midnight Cowboy*

702) "Everybody's Talkin" (Harry Nilsson)   b. *Pat Garrett and Billy the Kid*

703) "Knockin' on Heaven's Door" (Bob Dylan)   c. *The Sting*

704) "Colonel Bogey" (Mitch Miller)   d. *The Spy Who Loved Me*

705) "Nobody Does It Better" (Carly Simon)   e. *The Bridge on the River Kwai*

. . . Answers

696. Electric Light Orchestra

697. Little Richard

698. Jimi Hendrix

699. b

700. Miles Davis

701. c

702. a

703. b

704. e

705. d

706) Who was born Dellareese Talioferro?

707) What female vocalist portrayed the guitar-playing singing nun in the movie *Airport '75*?

708) According to *Cashbox*, what was the top single of 1967?
    a. "The Letter"
    b. "Windy"
    c. "The Unicorn"

709) "One," "Easy to Be Hard" and "Mama Told Me (Not to Come)" were some of the more than a dozen chartbusters of what group?

710) The 1955 hit "Maybellene" was recorded by what rock 'n' roller?

711) What rock group started out as the Golliwogs?

712) Whose first big hit came in 1966 with "When A Man Loves A Woman"?

713) What is the actual name of the group ELP?

714) True or false: Mick Jagger attended the London School of Economics.

715) Who performed the song and video "Dancing With Myself" which depicts the singer atop a skyscraper being attacked by zombies from a burned-out city?

. . . Answers

706. Della Reese

707. Helen Reddy

708. a

709. Three Dog Night

710. Chuck Berry

711. Creedence Clearwater Revival

712. Percy Sledge

713. Emerson, Lake and Palmer

714. True

715. Billy Idol

716) Who won two Grammy Awards for Best Inspirational Performance for "How Great Thou Art," in 1967 and 1974?

717) John Winston Lennon changed his middle name to what?

718) True or false: The Brotherhood was a spinoff of Paul Revere and the Raiders.

719) Name the clothes store owner who became manager for the Sex Pistols and in 1984 had his own hit and video with "Buffalo Girls."

720) True or false: *Billboard* magazine began publishing a weekly chart of the best-selling records of popular music in 1940.

721) What was Gilbert O'Sullivan's 1972 smash hit?
     a. "Alone Again (Naturally)"
     b. "Wheels A' Fire"
     c. "Camouflage"

722) Who recorded "Sock It to Me Baby" in 1967?

723) What rock group from Portland, Oregon recorded "Harden My Heart"?

724) What actor/singer played in both *Jesus Christ Superstar* and *Pippin*?

. . . Answers

716. Elvis Presley

717. Ono

718. True

719. Malcolm McLaren

720. True

721. a

722. Mitch Ryder and the Detroit Wheels

723. Quarterflash

724. Ben Vereen

725) Name Bobbie Gentry's hit song that was later made into a movie.

726) True or false: The lead singer for Them was Eric Clapton.

727) What performance artist, who is attuned to American catch phrases, recorded the album *Big Science* and the British hit single "O Superman"?

728) Who is Jessi Colter married to?

729) What leader of reggae music wrote and sang "No Woman No Cry" and "Lively Up Yourself"?

730) What black group was lead by Marilyn McCoo and Billy Davis?

731) What type of musical instrument is a high hat?

732) The song "Woman" was recorded by Peter and Gordon and written by Bernard Webb. Who was Bernard Webb?

733) True or false: Van Morrison wrote "Gloria" and "Brown Eyed Girl."

734) Who sang these historical songs: "The Battle of New Orleans," "North to Alaska" and "Sink the Bismarck"?

... *Answers*

725. "Ode to Billy Joe"

726. False

727. Laurie Anderson

728. Waylon Jennings

729. Bob Marley

730. The Fifth Dimension

731. Cymbals

732. Paul McCartney

733. True

734. Johnny Horton

35) What vocalist sang "Lovely Teenager" and "Run-round Sue"?

36) Emmylou Harris won the Country Music Award for Best Country Vocal Performance in 1976 with what album?

37) What famous folksinger was born in Hibbing, Minnesota?

38) True or false: "96 Tears" was originally performed by a singer whose legal name was ?

39) Michael Jackson's *Thriller* album, with sales of twenty-three million in early 1984, was fast approaching what double album soundtrack as the biggest worldwide seller?

40) Domingo Samudio and his band had a hit record in 1965 called "Wooly Bully." By what name is he better known?

41) How many piano keys are there inclusive from one C to the next C an octave lower?

42) What English group was originally known as the High Numbers?

43) On the album *The Real Thing*, who played, among other instruments, the amplified harp and the six-holed fife, backed up by a quartet of tubas?

. . . Answers

735. Dion

736. *Elite Hotel*

737. Bob Dylan

738. True

739. *Saturday Night Fever*

740. Sam the Sham

741. Thirteen

742. The Who

743. Taj Mahal

744) What won the Grammy for Best Country Song of 1976?

745) Who was the Beatles' manager that died from a drug and alcohol overdose?

746) Born Anthony Dominick Benedetto, he left his heart in San Francisco. What is his name?

747) What Massachusetts band had the hit "More Than A Feeling"?

748) In 1968 he released the album *Recital* in which he not only sang but played bass, piano, harpsichord and organ. He also arranged and wrote the songs. Name him.

749) Eddie, currently regarded as the hottest guitar player in the country, and his brother Alex are two members of the group with their last name. Name the group.

750) Thinking that this artist looked like a young Fats Domino, Mrs. Dick Clark gave what singer his stage name?

. . . Answers

744. "Broken Lady" by Larry Gatlin and the Gatlin Brothers Band

745. Brian Epstein

746. Tony Bennett

747. Boston

748. Lee Michaels

749. Van Halen

750. Chubby Checker

Match these one-word titles with the singers who recorded them

51) "Physical"   a. Roy Orbison

52) "Coconut"   b. Peggy Lee

53) "Sailing"   c. Barbra Streisand

54) "People"   d. Christopher Cross

55) "Fever"   e. Harry Nilsson

56) "Crying"   f. Olivia Newton-John

57) True or false: Boy George is an ex-member of Bow Wow Wow.

58) Name the composer, born in 1898, who died at the age of 38. He wrote his first song, "Since I Found You," at the age of 15. His last song was "Love Is Here to Stay."

59) Lowering the musical third of a major chord by a half step produces what chord?

60) What composer, with Johnny Burke Van Heusen, wrote most of Bing Crosby's songs from 1940 to 1952 and, with Sammy Cahn, most of Frank Sinatra's in subsequent years? He wrote scores for *The Bells of St. Mary's* and *A Connecticut Yankee in King Arthur's Court.*

61) Whose first hit in 1962 was the Bacharach-David song "Don't Make Me Over"?

. . . Answers

751. f

752. e

753. d

754. c

755. b

756. a

757. True

758. George Gershwin

759. A minor chord

760. Jimmy Van Heusen

761. Dionne Warwick

762) What was the theme song of Cab Calloway's band?

763) George Thorogood recorded the 1982 album *Bad to the Bone* with what group?

764) Who won an Elvis soundalike contest and recorded "Be-Bop-A-Lula" in 1956?

765) "Lalena" and "Atlantis" were hits from what Scottish vocalist?

766) What country group first played under the name the Kingsmen?

767) Who performed the hits "Breathless" and "Whole Lotta Shakin' Going On"?

768) In 1964 what group released the album *Glad All Over*?

769) Who sang the part of Tommy in the Who's opera with the London Symphony Orchestra?

770) Which country star married a female regular of the TV show *Hee-Haw*?

771) What conductor was born in Berlin, raised in California, and led the London Symphony for eleven years?

. . . Answers

762. "Minnie the Moocher"

763. George Thorogood and the Destroyers

764. Gene Vincent

765. Donovan

766. Statler Brothers

767. Jerry Lee Lewis

768. The Dave Clark Five

769. Roger Daltrey

770. Kenny Rogers

771. Andre Previn

QUESTIONS

72) What was the theme song of Rudy Vallee's band?

73) Eric Clapton had the hit "Layla" in 1972 with what group?

74) Of these top albums of 1968, which one was #1?
   a. *Are You Experienced?*
   b. *The Graduate*
   c. *Disraeli Gears*

75) True or false: The Thompson Twins are actually one black male, a white male and a white female.

76) Who wrote and recorded "Rock Around the Clock" which later became the theme for *Blackboard Jungle*?

77) Which is not a pedal on the piano?
   a. coupler
   b. damper
   c. sostenuto
   d. soft

78) Mark Lindsay sang lead for what American group?

79) Peter and Gordon scored in 1965 with "I Go To Pieces," written by what singer/writer who had his own major hit with "Runaway" in 1961?

. . . *Answers*

772. "My Time Is Your Time"

773. Derek And The Dominos

774. c

775. True

776. Bill Haley

777. a

778. Paul Revere and the Raiders

779. Del Shannon

780) True or false: Louise Cryer sang with Les Brown and His Band of Renown.

781) Bob B. Soxx and Blue Jeans didn't have the same success with "Chapel of Love" that what later New Orleans group did?

782) The press linked this female star up with Governor Jerry Brown of California. What was her name?

783) Who wrote Tom Rush's "The Circle Game" and Nazareth's "This Flight Tonight"?

784) According to *Cashbox*, what was the top single of 1966?
   a. "See You in September"
   b. "Ode to Billie Joe"
   c. "The Ballad of the Green Berets"

785) What did the name Three Dog Night represent?
   a. a rough evening of bar hopping
   b. an Eskimo weather report
   c. a ball game that lasted extra innings

786) In what year did Eric Burdon let all the old Animals go and emerge with a new group called Eric Burdon and the Animals?

787) Who was the drummer for the Mahavishnu Orchestra that later had a solo album *Spectrum*?

. . . Answers

780. False

781. The Dixie Cups

782. Linda Ronstadt

783. Joni Mitchell

784. c

785. b

786. 1966

787. Billy Cobham

788) Who had his biggest hit in 1969 when he wrote and recorded "Okie From Muskogee"?

789) Who was the Beatles' original drummer?

790) In 1967 who released his first album, entitled *Are You Experienced*?

791) True or false: "Take Five," Dave Brubeck's most famous piece, was written by Paul Desmond.

792) Name the English artist parodied by John Belushi in *National Lampoon Lemmings* and on *Saturday Night Live*.

793) What narrative vocalist did "Cat's in the Cradle"?

794) True or false: *Your Hit Parade* a network broadcast of the most popular songs of the week was first aired in 1935.

795) What British group had the successful hits and videos "Love My Way" (1982) and "The Ghost in You" (1984)?

796) What songwriter and recording star advertised for a wife in a newspaper? He also married his fiddler, then tried to divorce her. After she went into hiding he bought a full-page ad asking her to come back.

797) What group that began as a spinoff of the Grateful Dead recorded the 1972 LP *Powerglide*?

. . . Answers

788. Merle Haggard

789. Pete Best

790. Jimi Hendrix

791. True

792. Joe Cocker

793. Harry Chapin

794. True

795. The Psychedelic Furs

796. Buck Owens

797. The New Riders of The Purple Sage

798) Who was known as "The Singing Brakeman"?

799) What legendary rhythm and blues singer did "Ain't Nothing You Can Do" and "Turn on Your Love Light"?

800) Who wrote "Moon River" and "Days of Wine and Roses"?

Match these songs with the artists who recorded them

801) "Georgia on My Mind"

a. Neil Diamond

802) "Kentucky Woman"

b. Woody Guthrie

803) "Oklahoma Hills"

c. Ray Charles

804) "New York Mining Disaster 1941"

d. Mamas And Papas

805) "California Dreamin' "

e. Bee Gees

806) "Ohio"

f. Crosby, Stills, Nash and Young

807) In 1955, what was Little Richard's first hit?

808) Their song "Eight Miles High" was banned on some radio stations on the grounds that it glorified drugs. What was the name of this group?

. . . Answers

798. Jimmie Rodgers

799. Bobby "Blue" Bland

800. Henry Mancini

801. c

802. a

803. b

804. e

805. d

806. f

807. "Tutti Frutti"

808. The Byrds

309) Who were Jake and Elwood, lead singers and creators of the Blues Brothers?

310) Who wrote "Your Cheatin' Heart" and "I'm So Lonesome I Could Cry"?

311) Neil Diamond and the Hollies both had hits with what song?

312) Who was the singer and organist with the Blues Project who later formed Blood, Sweat and Tears? He made it big with the release of *Super Session*.

313) Dale Bozzio, ex-Playboy bunny and vocalist for Frank Zappa's "I Don't Want to Get Drafted", is the vocalist for what group?

314) True or false: Georgie Fame is best known for his release "The Ballad Of Bonnie and Clyde."

315) Who sold the greatest number of albums in 1966?
   a. Herb Alpert and the Tijuana Brass
   b. the Rolling Stones
   c. the Beatles
   d. Elvis Presley

316) Who was made "Dizzy" by "Sheila"?

317) Three musical notes played in the amount of time normally used for two notes are called what?

. . . *Answers*

809. John Belushi and Dan Aykroyd

810. Hank Williams

811. "He Ain't Heavy, He's My Brother"

812. Al Kooper

813. Missing Persons

814. True

815. a

816. Tommy Roe

817. Triplets

818) Who was only 13 when he recorded "Why Do Fools Fall in Love"?

819.) What was Bob James' sixth album?
   a. *Heads*
   b. *Touchdown*
   c. *Lucky Seven*

820) This singer and actress was born Frances Ethel Gumm in Grand Rapids, Michigan in 1922. She and her husband Sid Luft made their own movie *A Star Is Born*. In 1964 she appeared with her daughter in concert at the London Palladium. Who is she?

821) Where did the Bee Gees' lights go out?

822) Who was billed as "Oklahoma's Singing Cowboy." One of his hits was "Tumbling Tumbleweeds." He also owns the California Angels.

823) "Gimme Some Lovin' " and "I'm a Man" were hits for what British rhythm and blues band?

824) Who recorded "Mandy" and "I Write the Songs"?

825) Who built a bridge over troubled water?

826) What group recorded "Hang On Sloopy" in 1965 and later recorded the jazz-influenced "Resurrection"?

827) What female vocalist had a "Total Eclipse of the Heart"?

. . . Answers

818. Frankie Lymon

819. b

820. Judy Garland

821. "Massachusetts"

822. Gene Autry

823. Spencer Davis Group

824. Barry Manilow

825. Simon and Garfunkel

826. The McCoys

827. Bonnie Tyler

QUESTIONS

828) This musician's band, the Hawks, was made up of five men who would later back Bob Dylan and become known as the Band. What was his name?

829) Who had a slogan on his guitar that read "This Machine Kills Fascists"?
   a. Ray Charles
   b. Woody Guthrie
   c. B.B. King
   d. Howlin' Wolf

830) What singer is the daughter of Carl Smith and June Carter Cash?

831) What folk rocker created the film *Renaldo and Clara* in 1978?

832) She was born Constance Franconero in 1938. She was a winner on *Arthur Godfrey's Talent Scout* show. Name her.

833) What group's name came from Barry Gibb's initials?

834) What country artist claimed to have done his best singing from 1936 to 1939, before he had his tonsils removed? He recorded "Walking the Floor Over You."

835) Who was the slide guitarist for Derek and the Dominoes?

. . . Answers

828. Ronnie Hawkins

829. b

830. Carlene Carter

831. Bob Dylan

832. Connie Francis

833. The Bee Gees

834. Ernest Tubb

835. Duane Allman

836) How did Conway Twitty get his name?

837) What Swedish group reportedly earns more each year than the Volvo company?

838) Who was the first female country singer to have a million selling record, "I Want to Be a Cowboy's Sweetheart"?

839) What song, first done by Smokey Robinson and the Miracles, reached the top of the charts for both Gladys Knight and the Pips as well as Marvin Gaye?

840) Which musical group sang "Mendocino"?

841) What musical group did "You've Made Me So Very Happy" and "Variations on a Theme by Eric Satie"?

842) What musical play features the songs "Try to Remember" and "Soon It's Gonna Rain"?

843) True or false: Aretha Franklin's father, Rev. C. L. Franklin, has made over eighty albums of sermons.

844) What play won the Tony Award as the best musical play of 1970?

845) Who is the first pop star to have six singles from the same album reach the top ten?

. . . Answers

836. He took it from Conway, Arkansas and Twitty, Texas

837. Abba

838. Patsy Montana

839. "I Heard It Through the Grapevine"

840. The Sir Douglas Quintet

841. Blood, Sweat and Tears

842. "The Fantasticks"

843. True

844. *Company*

845. Michael Jackson

846) Who was named the Country Music Association's entertainer of the year in 1979?

847) After losing faith in one another, what short-lived super group of 1969 sold a million copies of their only album?

848) Who was the original Harold Hill in the Broadway musical *The Music Man* in 1957?

849) What song from "Jesus Christ Superstar" launched Helen Reddy's career?

850) The first American musical was performed in what year?
   a. 1852
   b. 1866
   c. 1882

Match the group with its leader

851) Patti Labelle   a. the Pacemakers

852) Prince   b. the Raiders

853) Sly   c. the Revolution

854) Archie Bell   d. the Bluebelles

855) Paul Revere   e. the Family Stone

856) Gerry   f. the Blackhearts

857) Joan Jett   g. the Drells

. . . Answers

846. Willie Nelson

847. Blind Faith

848. Robert Preston

849. "I Don't Know How to Love Him"

850. b

851. d

852. c

853. e

854. g

855. b

856. a

857. f

858) Name Martha Reeves' hot Motown group.

859) True or false: "Your Hit Parade" switched from radio to television in 1957.

860) The Nice was the original band of what keyboard artist?
   a. Stevie Wonder
   b. Ike Turner
   c. Keith Emerson
   d. Alan Parsons

861) What English folksinger released her first single "As Tears Go By" in 1964? She also appeared in the film *Girl on a Motorcycle*.

862) Antonio Stradivari is best known for what musical contribution?

863) Who was Big Brother and the Holding Company's lead vocalist after Janis Joplin?

864) What rock band was America's answer to the Beatles doing such greats as "Turn Turn Turn" and "Mr. Tambourine Man"?

865) True or false: Mickey Rooney, Sr. recorded two singles with his sons in 1967.

866) What British group did "(Wish I Could Fly Like) Superman" in 1979?

. . . Answers

858. Martha and the Vandellas

859. False

860. c

861. Marianne Faithful

862. Stradivarius violins

863. Nick Gravenites

864. The Byrds

865. False

866. The Kinks

367) All they are is "Dust in the Wind." Who are they?

368) What songwriter sang of meeting his former girlfriend while driving a taxi?

369) What do the musicals *Godspell* and *Jesus Christ Superstar* have in common?

370) In 1965 who sang the title song to the James Bond movie *Goldfinger*?

371) Whose frailing banjo could be heard on the TV show *Hee-Haw* for many years?

372) What song is Little Peggy March's claim to fame?

373) The album *Switched On Bach* featured what instrument?

374) What German group performs the anti-nuclear song "99 Luftballoons"?
   a. Kraftwerk   c. Trio
   b. Nena   d. Lederhosen

375) The film and play *Two for the Seesaw* was turned into what musical play in 1973?

376) Who are "the bad boys of rock 'n' roll"?

377) Who was the founder and force behind Sun Records of Memphis?

. . . Answers

867. Kansas

868. Harry Chapin

869. Both were based on the Bible, Book of Matthew

870. Shirley Bassey

871. Grandpa Jones

872. "I Will Follow Him"

873. Moog synthesizer

874. b

875. *Seesaw*

876. The Rolling Stones

877. Sam Phillips

78) What New Orleans composer-singer found his thrill on Blueberry Hill?

79) What Maine musician was known for his trucking music with such tunes as "Tombstone Every Mile" and "Six Days on the Road"?

80) Stereophonic records were first commercially available to the public in what year?
   a. 1948   c. 1962
   b. 1958   d. 1965

81) What singer was with Buddy Holly and Richie Valens when their plane went down on February 3, 1959?

82) What blues band made the album *Golden Butter*?

83) This group had thirty-five changes in personnel in three years before they made it late in 1968. Their lead guitarist was Ted Nugent. What was their name?

84) "Crazy Mama" and "After Midnight" were written and sung by what laid-back blues performer?

85) In the early sixties Rudy Lewis sang lead for this group as they recorded "Up on the Roof" and "On Broadway." Name the group.

86) Holland/Dozier/Holland was a Motown song-writing team that formed what label in 1968?

. . . Answers

878. Fats Domino

879. Dick Curless

880. b

881. The Big Bopper (J.P. Richardson)

882. The Paul Butterfield Blues Band

883. The Amboy Dukes

884. J.J. Cale

885. The Drifters

886. Invictus/Hot Wax

87) Who was born Bobby Villine in 1943?

88) What female vocalist is the granddaughter of German Nobel Prize-winner Max Born?

89) Who did the Country Music Association honor as the vocal duo of the year in 1978 and 1979?

90) Which Allman brother was killed in a motorcycle crash in 1971?

91) Who released the international hit "A Groovy Kind of Love" in 1966?

92) What master of the guitar formed the Mahavishnu Orchestra and also performed *Love, Devotion, Surrender* with Carlos Santana?

93) This musical was a Broadway play and later a movie. It opened at the Winter Garden Theater in New York City in March 1964. It was based on the life of a singer and comedian played by Barbra Streisand. Name it.

94) What brother group has written more than one thousand published songs?

95) Which country star at the age of ten formed his first group, the Phillips County Ramblers?

. . . Answers

887. Bobby Vee

888. Olivia Newton-John

889. Dottie West and Kenny Rogers

890. Duane Allman

891. The Mindbenders

892. John McLaughlin

893. *Funny Girl*

894. The Bee Gees

895. Conway Twitty

396) True or false: There is an overabundance of conductors to supply the world's opera companies and orchestras.

397) What English group recorded "We Gotta Get Out of This Place"?

398) What vocal quartet did "Young Blood" and "Poison Ivy"?

899) Brewer and Shipley's only hit record ran into censorship problems because it was about marijuana. Name the song.

900) His first name in Carlos. His last name is the same as his group.

Match these anti-nuclear songs and videos with the artists who perform them

901) "Distant Early Warning"   a. Men at Work

902) "Stop in the Name of Love"   b. The Fixx

903) "It's a Mistake"   c. Donald Fagen

904) "Stand or Fall"   d. Rush

905) "New Frontier"   e. The Hollies

. . . *Answers*

896. False

897. The Animals

898. The Coasters

899. "One Toke Over the Line"

900. Santana

901. d

902. e

903. a

904. b

905. c

QUESTIONS

906) What performer started in the business with his father and uncles when he was four, lost his left eye in an automobile crash in 1954, and sings "Mr. Wonderful" and "Without You"?

907) Bing Crosby's 1982 hit single "Peace on Earth" was a dub performed with whom?
    a. Rosemary Clooney
    b. Dean Martin
    c. David Bowie

908) What group recorded "Born on the Bayou" in 1969?

909) What American songwriter and singer had a #1 hit in England with a song about Vincent Van Gogh?

910) Jim Morrison sang lead for what group?

911) Who brought America aboard the "Love Train"?

912) What musical play, brought over from England in the early 60's, featured the big musical number, "What Kind of Fool Am I"?

913) What scholar, philosopher and organist wrote the book *J. S. Bach, Musician and Poet*?

914) Name the son of a famous comedian who released "This Diamond Ring" in 1965?

. . . Answers

906. Sammy Davis, Jr.

907. c

908. Creedence Clearwater Revival

909. Don McLean

910. The Doors

911. The O'Jays

912. "Stop the World—I Want to Get Off"

913. Albert Schweitzer

914. Gary Lewis

915) In the US, a gold album is one that has sold at least what?
  a. one million dollars worth of records
  b. one hundred hundred thousand copies
  c. five thousand copies
  d. one million copies

916) Dale Evans sang for what big band?

917) Travers, Yarrow and Stookey formed what well-known trio?

918) What group's primary claim to fame was that its lead singer, Grace Slick, went on to sing with Jefferson Airplane?

919) Which of the following is not a member of the woodwind family?
  a. oboe
  b. bassoon
  c. English horn
  d. French horn

920) Who had the hits "Maybe I Know" (1964) and "California Nights" (1967)?

921) Which of the following is not a bowed, string instrument?
  a. crwth
  b. adze
  c. viola
  d. double bass

. . . Answers

915. c

916. Anson Weeks'

917. Peter, Paul and Mary

918. The Great Society

919. d

920. Lesley Gore

921. b

922) This group was one of the first New York groups (they came from the Bronx) to play psychedelic rock. Their first album *Psychedelic Lollipop* was recorded late in 1966. Name them.

923) Kim Carnes and Kenny Rogers were part of what folk-pop group?

924) True or false: The Association's hit "Along Comes Mary" was actually banned in some places for having second-meaning lyrics and "drug slang."

925) In 1966 they fought the law, but the law won. Name them.

926) In 1947, who headlined the first country show at Carnegie Hall?

927) Who recorded the album *Beautiful Noise*, produced by the Band's Robbie Robertson?

928) What do Leslie Uggams, Joe Tex and James Brown have in common?
   a. All started in the business in 1956
   b. All got their start by performing Harlem's Apollo Theater
   c. All grew up in the same town

929) His first two names are Harry Lillis, and he has sold over four hundred million records. Name this crooner.

. . . Answers

922. The Blues Magoos

923. The New Christy Minstrels

924. False

925. The Bobby Fuller Four

926. Ernest Tubb

927. Neil Diamond

928. b

929. Bing Crosby

930) Who is known as "Mr. Guitar"?

931) What British group did "Feel Like Makin' Love" and "Rock and Roll Fantasy"?

932) Whose first album was entitled *Pandemonium Shadow Show*?

933) What group anonymously recorded Bob Dylan's "Don't Think Twice, It's Alright" under the pseudonym Wonder Who in 1965?

934) This multi-talented personality played Mary Poppins and Maria von Trapp. Who is she?

935) What soul band did the instrumental hit "Time Is Tight" in 1969 and was featured in *The Blues Brothers* movie?

936) Doris Day sang with which big band?

937) What female vocalist sang "Midnight at the Oasis" in 1974?

938) What band leader surrounded himself with a bevy of female musicians in his *Hour of Charm* radio series?

939) Michael McDonald was the vocalist for what group with hits "Take Me in Your Arms (Rock Me)" and "Takin' It to the Streets"?

. . . Answers

930. Chet Atkins

931. Bad Company

932. Harry Nilsson

933. The Four Seasons

934. Julie Andrews

935. Booker T. and the MGs

936. Les Brown's

937. Maria Muldaur

938. Phil Spitalny

939. The Doobie Brothers

940) What female singer joined the Flying Burrito Brothers only to have the group break up one week later?

941) Who wrote Peter, Paul and Mary's socially conscious hit "If I Had a Hammer"?

942) What singer made his screen debut with Clint Eastwood in *Every Which Way But Loose*?

943) In what city did the Motown studios originate?

944) Which of the following plays was about the rise of the Nazis in pre-war Berlin?
    a. *Can Can*
    b. *Brigadoon*
    c. *Cabaret*

945) What ex-Beatles sideman had a hit of his own in 1972 with "Outa Space"?

946) Two former members of John Mayall's Bluesbreakers with the same first name formed what jazz-folk group named for their surnames?

947) The 1966 Phil Spector-produced single "River Deep, Mountain High" was performed by what group?

948) This singer didn't think much of short people.

. . . Answers

940. Emmylou Harris

941. Peter Seeger and Lee Hays

942. Charlie Pride

943. Detroit

944. c

945. Billy Preston

946. The Mark-Almond Band

947. Ike and Tina Turner

948. Randy Newman

949) Mick Fleetwood and John McVie moved from John Mayall's Bluesbreakers to form what long-lived group?

950) During the early 1960s what group backed up Dion?

Match the musical with its source.

951) *Autumn's Here*	a. *The Time of the Cuckoo*
952) *Do I Hear a Waltz?*	b. *The Legend of Sleepy Hollow*
953) *Girl Called Joe*	c. *The Princess and the Pea*
954) *Once Upon a Mattress*	d. *A Midsummer Night's Dream*
955) *Swingin' the Dream*	e. *Little Women*

956) The mouth organ is a free-reed instrument better known as what?

957) What actress starred in the musical play *Applause*?

958) What reggae singer is gonna rock onto "Electric Avenue" before "Romancing the Stone"?

959) What folk-rock group recorded Bacharach-David's "My Little Red Book" in 1966?
    a. Love   c. The Doors
    b. Byrds

. . . Answers

949. Fleetwood Mac

950. The Belmonts

951. b

952. a

953. e

954. c

955. d

956. Harmonica

957. Lauren Bacall

958. Eddy Grant

959. a

960) Who recorded the fifties hit "Chantilly Lace"?

961) What was the name of the Puerto Rican gang in the musical *West Side Story*?

962) Who wrote "There's Always Something There to Remind Me," a #1 British hit for Sandie Shaw?

963) What was the theme song of Ozzie Nelson's band?

964) Guitarist Mark Knopfler wrote the score for the film *Local Hero*. Name his group which had the 1979 hit "Sultans of Swing."

965) Two members of Crosby, Stills, Nash and Young were first part of this group. Two other members of this group formed the country-rock group, Poco. They recorded their first album in 1967. Name this group.

966) What female singer wrote two songs and sang on Blue Oyster Cult's album *Agents of Fortune*?

967) She was discovered by Bill Anderson in the sixties. Her first record in 1964, "Once a Day," was a #1 hit. Name her.

968) This British group of the 1960s had many hits in England, but only "Itchycoo Park" was successful in America. Name them.

. . . Answers

960. The Big Bopper

961. Sharks

962. Burt Bacharach

963. "Loyal Sons of Rutgers"

964. Dire Straits

965. Buffalo Springfield

966. Patti Smith

967. Connie Smith

968. The Small Faces

969) True or false: Three of Mickey Rooney's sons recorded under the name the Rooney Brothers.

970) Pat Boone made his musical debut on what TV show during the fifties, emceed by Arthur Godfrey?

971) Rosemary Clooney sang for what big band?

972) What folksinger's bare breast on the album cover *Buffy* caused consternation in the early seventies?

973) Which of the original Supremes was married?

974) What folksinger helped make a film about Antonia Bricas, her former piano teacher?

975) This black performer was a master showman of the sixties. His hits include "I Got You (I Feel Good)" and "It's a Man's, Man's, Man's World." Name him.

976) Who had the hit single "Pictures of Matchstick Men"?

977) Born Virginia Patterson Hensley in 1932 in Virginia, she became the first country female singer to achieve stardom on her own rather than by appearing as the female attraction on a male star's package show. Name her.

978) Donovan performed his 1969 hit "Goo Goo Barabajagal" with what British guitarist?

. . . Answers

969. True

970. *Talent Scouts*

971. Tony Pastor's

972. Buffy Sainte-Marie

973. Florence Ballard

974. Judy Collins

975. James Brown

976. Status Quo

977. Patsy Cline

978. Jeff Beck

979) She is married to Johnny Cash. Johnny and she did a duet called "Jackson." She came from a musical family and was part of a family country group. What is her name?

980) What lead singer whose group did "Love Her Madly" was arrested for indecent exposure on stage in 1969?

981) Which country entertainer contracted malaria which left him with a speech impairment in 1932?

982) What singer saw "fire and rain" in 1970?

983) In 1970 Richard Rodgers collaborated with Martin Charnin and returned to the theatre with a play called what?

984) Her 1971 LP, *Live at Fillmore West*, included a duet with Ray Charles. Who is she?

985) Who is known for the tunes "Please Help Me, I'm Falling" and "Send Me the Pillow You Dream On"?

986) In what Billy Joel video did his girlfriend Christie Brinkley appear?

987) From what musical play did these tunes come: "What Is This Thing Called Love?" and "Let's Do It"?

. . . Answers

979. June Carter Cash

980. Jim Morrison

981. Mel Tillis

982. James Taylor

983. *Two by Two*

984. Aretha Franklin

985. Hank Locklin

986. "Uptown Girl"

987. *Wake Up and Dream*

988) Buxtehude's seventeenth century Abendmusik concerts were performed at what time of day?

989) She was four foot, seven inches tall with a brassy voice. She started in the business in the late 50's. One of her big hits was "Sweet Nothings." Name her.

990) Name the all-girl group who's "got the beat."

991) True or false: The Statler Brothers are really brothers.

992) "This Masquerade" was a gold record for George Benson, but earlier it was on the gold album *Carney*, performed by the song's writer. Who wrote it?

993) What musician and TV personality owned his own barber shop at the age of fifteen?

994) True or false: The Burmese, mohawk-haired singer of Bow Wow Wow, Annabella Lwin, was discovered by former Sex Pistols manager Malcolm McLaren in a London launderette.

995) Who's the backup group for Prince?

996) What is the distinguishing characteristic of music performed a capella?

. . . Answers

988. Evening

989. Brenda Lee

990. The Go-Go's

991. False

992. Leon Russell

993. Perry Como

994. True

995. The Revolution

996. It is vocal without instrumental accompaniment

997) Under what name did Mr. Stuart and Mr. Clyde record "Mr. Tambourine Man"?

998) What Berkeley group did "Fortunate Son" and "Bad Moon Rising"?

999) True or false: Singer Fred Neil ran a promotion: Buy one Fred Neil record and get one free.

1000) Name the one-time Beach Boys lyricist who recorded the album Jump in 1984.

1001) What was Sonny and Cher's first hit?

1002) What is Paul McCartney's real first name?

. . . Answers

997. Chad and Jeremy

998. Creedence Clearwater Revival

999. True

1000. Van Dyke Parks

1001. "I Got You Babe"

1002. James